FIONA PEEK

Fiona Peek graduated with a BA Hons in English and Philosophy from Trinity College, Cambridge. She worked for many years as an actress and director in Cork, Ireland, before returning to England and, in 2006, completing an MA in Dramatic Writing at Sussex University. She currently combines writing with motherhood and lives in Brighton with her husband and two young children.

Fiona Peek

SALT

NICK HERN BOOKS

London

www.nickhernbooks.co.uk

A Nick Hern Book

Salt first published in Great Britain as a paperback original in 2010 by Nick Hern Books Limited, 14 Larden Road, London W3 7ST

Salt copyright © 2010 Fiona Peek

Fiona Peek has asserted her right to be identified as the author of this work

Cover image: © iStockphoto.com/mattjeacock
Cover design: Ned Hoste, 2H

Typeset by Nick Hern Books, London
Printed in Great Britain by CLE Print Ltd, St Ives, Cambs PE27 3LE

A CIP catalogue record for this book is available from the British Library

ISBN   978 1 84842 069 4

This book is printed on FSC-accredited paper made from trees from sustainable forests.

Salt was first performed in the Studio at the Royal Exchange Theatre, Manchester, on 3 February 2010, with the following cast:

SIMON	Simon Chadwick
NICK	Kevin Harvey
AMY	Beth Cordingly
RACHEL	Esther Hall

Director   Jo Combes
Designer   Ben Stones
Lighting Designer   Richard Owen
Sound Designer   Gerry Marsden

In memory of
Roy Arthur Paul Peek

With love and heartfelt thanks to
Margaret,
Mike and Liz,
and
My beautiful Shaggy

'To curb ambition I crave salt and fat'

Suzy Willson

'Civilisation cannot survive without salt'

New Scientist

Characters

SIMON, *forty-one*
NICK, *thirty-eight*
AMY, *thirty-eight*
RACHEL, *forty*

This text went to press before the end of rehearsals and so may differ slightly from the play as performed.

Scene One

A state-of-the-art kitchen, with a table, middle stage-right. The table is distorted, more rhomboid than square.

Each scene of the play takes place during a different course of a different meal. Whatever the stage of that meal, the table is laid accordingly by the actors at the beginning of the scene. This preparation takes place to music and has a ritualistic quality to it. In Scene One, it takes the form of a spinning, chaotic dance, dishes appearing as if by magic from left and right. The result is a table set in disarray, the remains of a main course – plates, a half-finished salad – alongside a desecrated cheeseboard, spilt wine, etc. Three empty wine bottles are littered around and a fourth sits on the table, half full.

Much laughter and indecipherable 'chat' accompanies the action.

Only when the preparation is complete, does the scene begin.

As the characters come to rest, AMY *is seated at the table talking to* NICK, *whilst absent-mindedly gathering together the plates and remains of food.* SIMON *is hunched over what turns out to be the oven, talking to the pudding.*

RACHEL *is absent.*

SIMON (*to the pudding*). Come on, baby. Come to Papa!

NICK (*to* AMY). Cash flow.

SIMON. Easy now…

NICK. So of course, I'm thinking…

SIMON. No.

NICK. …clearly they're about to go under.

SIMON. No. No!

NICK. I can relate to that.

SIMON. Oops!

NICK. Anyhow, I swan on in there, ladling out the condolences…

Holding it with a tea towel, SIMON *eases the pudding from the oven.*

SIMON. That's the way…

NICK. Turns out… it's just me getting screwed.

SIMON. Yes!

NICK. They've been pipped at the post with the article…

SIMON (*sniffing the tin as he straightens*). Mmmm…

NICK. They don't want it any more.

AMY. And the fact that it's what they commissioned?

SIMON (*to the pudding*). Hello, beautiful!

NICK. Totally fucking irrelevant.

SIMON *looks around for somewhere to deposit the tin. It contains something that resembles a chocolate soufflé with a pastry base.*

AMY (*to* NICK). Unbelievable!

The tin is clearly starting to burn SIMON.

SIMON. Aargh!

AMY (*to* NICK). Poor baby! After all that work…

SIMON (*plaintively*). Ames?

AMY *moves swiftly towards him, picking up a pair of oven gloves from the back of a chair as she goes. She's used to this.*

AMY (*taking the tin from* SIMON). Oh well, stuff them. They still have to pay you.

SIMON *hops from foot to foot, clutching his finger.*

NICK. No! No, no. In fact, they were most specific on that
point.

AMY. What?

NICK. Company policy.

AMY. But…

AMY turns on the tap for SIMON *with her free hand.*

(*To* SIMON.) Cold tap, honey.

NICK. We're two a penny, apparently. They told me so.

AMY. That's outrageous! What about your contract?

SIMON sighs with relief as he plunges his hand under the tap.

Pause.

Oh, Nick…

NICK. It's never mattered before!

AMY. Well, what did you say to them?

AMY looks for somewhere to deposit the tin.

(*To* SIMON.) Si, darling?

*SIMON looks at the tin and back at his hand and scratches
his head. He turns off the tap and picks up two tea towels
this time. Taking care to double them over, he takes the tin
from* AMY.

(*To* NICK.) Did you say anything?

Throughout the following exchange SIMON *performs a swift
but elaborate comic dumbshow, as he fetches a board on
which to place the tin, a spatula and a serving plate, all the
while carrying the pudding around the kitchen with him and
humming to himself as he does so. He eases the base out of
the tin and places the pudding carefully on the board. The
remainder of the tin, which is now around his forearm,
begins to burn him. He removes it hurriedly and prises the
tart away from the base with the spatula.*

NICK. I told them that their mothers were camels' whores and that their dicks could pass through the eyes of needles. Or some such.

Beat.

I'm giving up journalism. Think I'll stick to the carpentry.

Pause.

Rachel's gonna have a coronary.

AMY. You should get Si on to it...

They look at SIMON *who is struggling to hold onto everything.*

Or not.

NICK. You know what gets me? That after all these years of playing them at their own game, I never saw it coming.

Beat.

'Nick, you unprincipled cunt!'

Beat.

'We know you're deep in the shit. We can smell your fear...'

AMY. Rachel's been gone a while...

NICK. 'Clearly you're the man for the job!'

AMY. Nick?

NICK. 'Wait a minute!'

AMY. Nick?

NICK. 'Hold fire. Change of plan...'

AMY. NICK!

SIMON *slides the pudding onto the serving dish.*

SIMON. YES!!

NICK. WHAT? Rachel's fine!

AMY *rolls her eyes at him.*

She's fine!

SIMON *holds the pudding aloft in triumph as* RACHEL *enters.*

SIMON. And they said it was all over!

RACHEL. What was?

SIMON *jumps and mimes nearly dropping the pudding.*

SIMON. Woah!

RACHEL. Sorry.

SIMON. There you are!

He gives her a bear hug, still holding onto the pudding.

We thought you'd left us!

RACHEL. That looks fab!

AMY. You all right, lovely?

RACHEL. I'm fine! I'm fine. Sam says he wants water.

AMY. What! Is he not asleep?

AMY *fills a cup from the tap.*

SIMON *places the pudding on the work surface and fetches a bottle of dessert wine from the rack.*

RACHEL. He's making a time bomb, apparently.

SIMON. Oh Christ.

He begins opening the bottle.

AMY. I'll go.

She exits.

SIMON. She's a marvel, that woman.

RACHEL. She really is. I'm tired just looking at her.

SIMON. Well, you know Ames – all or nothing.

SIMON *goes hunting for dessert wine glasses.* RACHEL *looks for bowls.*

NICK. How the hell do you make a time bomb, anyway?

RACHEL. You should probably ask Sam that. He seems pretty confident.

SIMON (*groaning*). Ohhh.

NICK. I wonder how he's planning to detonate… Got your mobile, Simon?

SIMON*'s hand goes instinctively to his pocket.*

Ha! And from the home of inspired parenting…!

SIMON. I can always have you put away, you know, old boy. One call. All it takes.

Beat.

You don't really think he's got hold of anything, do you…?

NICK. What? Like Semtex?

RACHEL. What kind of thing?

SIMON. I don't know. What do they use?

NICK. Bleach? Batteries…? Drain cleaner?

Pause.

SIMON *goes to check the cupboard.*

Seriously – inspired.

RACHEL. I'm sure it's okay. There was no sign of anything like that.

NICK. And it's like a million to one against him getting his proportions right first time anyway.

Pause.

Unless, of course, he's got his greasy mitts on a recipe…

RACHEL. Nick! Stop it.

SIMON. Uh. I wouldn't put it past the little bugger.

NICK. The Belsize Bomber!

RACHEL. I really don't think you need worry.

NICK. Nah! We'll vouch for you with Social Services, won't we, Rach?

RACHEL (*to* SIMON). Just ignore him – he goes away.

NICK. So long as no one brings up the poisoning incident, eh?

SIMON (*gloomily*). And all those trips to casualty.

NICK. Ouch.

RACHEL. Anyway, I got the impression with this particular bomb that he was relying more on… the element of surprise.

AMY (*offstage*). Bloody hell!

AMY pounds down the stairs, bursts in, exasperated, and dumps a small pile of screws and metal in the centre of the table.

SIMON. What's that?

AMY. It's Granddad's watch.

SIMON. Ah. It appears to have been deconstructed.

AMY. I'm afraid I lost the plot slightly.

They look at her.

I've banned football.

SIMON. What, for ever?

NICK. So that's how you make a time bomb!

AMY. No. I don't know. For a bit.

SIMON pokes at the pile with his spoon.

It was the only family thing I gave a shit about.

SIMON. I can fix that.

Beat.

What? I can!

They stare at the pile in the middle of the table.

Pause.

NICK. I'll get the pudding then, shall I?

He goes to fetch the pudding. With a sigh, AMY *follows him, taking a jug of cream from the fridge and a serving spoon from the drawer.*

RACHEL. I'm sorry. I didn't realise it was so special.

SIMON. Nothing you could have done. Single-minded. Like his mother.

RACHEL *gently rakes the pile of screws and springs off the table and into her pudding bowl, which she places carefully on the work surface. She fetches another bowl for her pudding.*

Right then, folks! Grub's up.

They pull up chairs in a haphazard fashion as NICK *deposits the pudding on the table.*

Ah, ah. Gently does it.

SIMON *proffers the bottle of dessert wine.*

Rach?

RACHEL *covers her glass and gives a tiny shake of the head. Her previous wine glass is still half full.* AMY *glances at her thoughtfully, then turns to* NICK.

AMY (*to* NICK). So. What happened with that couple? The ones Kate put you on to?

RACHEL *looks at* NICK, *who shrugs ill-naturedly.*

RACHEL. Oh, they didn't need that much done in the end, did they, my love? Just a few shelves, that kind of thing. Cosmetic.

AMY (*to* NICK). Nick! You ungrateful old git.

NICK starts to laugh.

At least it's money.

NICK snorts.

SIMON (*to* RACHEL, *conspiratorially*). Teaching okay?

AMY (*to* NICK). I give it five years. Maximum.

She thumps NICK.

RACHEL (*to* SIMON). Loving it!

AMY (*to* NICK). Before you're completely unbearable.

RACHEL (*to* SIMON). Holidays, though.

NICK (*to* AMY). Five? Result.

RACHEL (*to* SIMON). Five long weeks, nearly six.

AMY (*to* NICK). You won't know any of us any more. We're all going to have abandoned you.

RACHEL (*to* SIMON). Lean times.

NICK (*to* AMY). I'm cuddly on the inside.

RACHEL (*to* SIMON). No one wants to be stuck inside, practising arpeggios when there's sun to be worshipped.

SIMON (*to* RACHEL). Hmm.

Beat.

RACHEL. At least Nick's still doing the odd article.

NICK. Great-looking pud. What is it?

SIMON looks around the table and down at the pudding. He raises a spoon.

SIMON. Listen…

Silence.

Very slowly, he lowers the spoon and with a swift tap, breaks the crust on the soufflé.

RACHEL. Oh!

NICK. Aaahh…

AMY. Off with its head!

RACHEL. It's not…?

SIMON. It is.

> RACHEL *moans.* NICK *slips his arms around her.*

NICK. Aw. My little cocoa fiend… Is that real pastry?

> SIMON *nods.*

What? You made it? No fucker makes pastry any more.

SIMON. Try it.

> NICK *breaks a piece off and tastes it.*

NICK. My God. It's like pure butter.

AMY. Well, I don't care what they say, I think it's great that the two of you are so at ease with your masculinity.

> SIMON *and* NICK *grin at one another.* NICK *gives* SIMON *a suggestive wink.*

> SIMON *starts to serve the pudding.*

SIMON. I suppose at least you get to enjoy the sunshine, eh?

RACHEL. Hmm. There's only so much weather a girl can take. I think I'd rather have the money right now.

> SIMON *helps her to pudding.*

NICK. Won't be long, lover. The Booker Man beckons.

RACHEL (*laughing*). Yum. Thank you.

SIMON (*helping* AMY *to pudding*). Aha! Near to finishing then?

NICK. Eight weeks? Give or take.

SIMON. Good Lord! That's bloody marvellous!

NICK. We'll be oozing into our award frocks before you can say 'Richard and Judy'…

SIMON. Oops!

SIMON leaps from his seat to fetch a bowl from the work surface.

NICK (*to* AMY)....*Then* you'll want to know me.

RACHEL. Si, this looks gorgeous.

SIMON. Why, thank you, beautiful!

AMY. Is that eight Earth weeks?

NICK. Fuck off.

SIMON. Oh, you of little faith. We're supping with genius, don't you know.

He delivers the bowl to the table with a flourish.

RACHEL. Ooh, raspberries! For optimism!

SIMON raises his glass to NICK.

SIMON. Excellent news, fella!

NICK. My number-one fan...

SIMON helps NICK and then himself to pudding.

Ta.

AMY. I know what I'm talking about.

NICK. No you don't! You're just a bitter... premenopausal old bag, who... God, this is fantastic!

AMY (*eating*). Uh-uh. That's it. Let's rewind a bit, shall we? Hmmm, let me see. December... '89? Yeah. Picture, if you will, the scene: It's three days – *three days* – before our final dissertation's due in and I'm huddled over a hot-water bottle in the worst student hovel known to woman, putting the finishing touches to my masterpiece, when in bursts Nick in what I can only describe as a... frenzy of outrage... This really is amazing, Si.

SIMON mimes an elaborate kiss in her direction.

RACHEL. Mmmnn...! Half-and-half...?

SIMON. Aha!

He pauses dramatically.

NICK. Sixty-five, thirty-five.

SIMON *mimes horror at* NICK's *correct guess.*

AMY *looks from one to the other in bewilderment.*

RACHEL. Proportions.

NICK. Dark to milk.

Beat.

AMY. Anyway! A third of a bottle of brandy later, it emerges that he's been into the library to borrow the two books he thinks *might* form the basis for a dissertation he thinks he *might* want to write and they've told him that they're in Wetherfield and will take twenty-four hours to be dispatched.

RACHEL. I didn't know Wetherfield was a real place.

AMY. It might have been Wetherby, actually. Or Wivelsfield, in fact. You'd think I'd remember that, though...

NICK. Your point being?

AMY. ...my point being that if it takes you a year and a day to borrow a book, the prospect of you actually completing one, in fact, of you achieving anything beyond tying your own shoelace in the space of the next eight weeks, fills me with a... curious excitement.

NICK. Why, you little...

He starts to poke her in the ribs repeatedly.

I'll show you!

It develops into full-blown tickling. They fall about giggling.

AMY. Aaargh! Simon!

SIMON. Oh no. Don't come crying to me. I'm revered for my impartiality.

NICK. I'll prove you wrong, dammit! (*With a maniacal laugh*.) I'll prove them all wrong!

NICK and AMY end up on the floor, crying with laughter. The other two continue to eat, looking on with amusement.

RACHEL. You did okay, though, didn't you?

NICK. Ah, but not as well as Amy…

NICK mouths the word 'First'.

RACHEL. Really?

AMY nods reluctantly, tidying herself up.

Wow! You've never mentioned that.

NICK. …for precision hole-punching.

AMY. Uh!

She begins thumping him repeatedly on the arm.

NICK. See! Genius.

A tussle ensues, at the end of which they break apart. AMY lies on the floor looking at NICK, who is sitting up. They're getting their breath back.

SIMON. Met a woman the other day…

NICK. You wanna watch that.

SIMON. …whose great-grandfather brought the first truly modern compensation case.

NICK. Bastard. Hate him.

SIMON. On the contrary, dear Watson. Something of a hero. A forefather of legal aid.

RACHEL. What was the case?

SIMON. A snail. In a bottle of ginger beer. In a 'caff'.

NICK. Can't see he's got much to complain about.

They laugh.

SIMON. An unfortunate *lady* by the name of… Donoghue, part-way through a beverage purchased for her by her more affluent companion, came across the remnants of said gastropod in her glass. *Cochlea decompositus*. Most unpleasant.

RACHEL. Oh God, the poor thing!

NICK *and* AMY *look at her.*

The woman, I mean.

SIMON (*reaching for* AMY*'s dish*). You want the rest of this?

AMY (*scrambling to her feet*). Yes, I do!

SIMON *picks up the serving spoon and begins helping himself to a substantial second portion of pudding.*

SIMON. Somewhat ironically, had she purchased the drink herself, there would have been no problem, but as things were – with no contract and no established duty of care – neither she nor the snail had a foot to stand on…

NICK *gets up.*

Any more for any more?

RACHEL *and* AMY *shake their heads.*

NICK *wobbles* SIMON*'s tummy on his way back to his seat.*

NICK. You porker!

SIMON. Oi, oi, oi!

SIMON *begins to eat.*

Anyway, solicitor didn't charge her a penny to bring the case…

He groans in pleasure at the food.

AMY. And?

SIMON. Huh? Oh, and they won. Eventually. All hypothetical, of course. But big money.

RACHEL. Wow. I wonder what happened to her.

SIMON. She died. Poverty-stricken. A few years later.

NICK. Oh Christ.

SIMON. Drank herself to death on the proceeds.

AMY. Nick! You're *not* going to die poverty-stricken!

SIMON. Just let me at him.

NICK grins and picks up a wine bottle.

NICK. Vino?

SIMON (*taking the bottle from* NICK). My apologies, old man.
Here.

He helps NICK *to wine, tops up* AMY*'s glass, glances at*
RACHEL*'s, and puts the bottle down.*

AMY. Coffee.

She goes to the espresso machine and begins to empty it out.

RACHEL. Do you have any herbal?

AMY looks at her. RACHEL *holds her gaze for a second
then looks away.*

AMY. Yes, of course. Ginger, fennel, detox, jasmine…

She goes to put on the kettle.

RACHEL. Goodness.

NICK. Bleeah…

RACHEL. Sorry.

NICK and RACHEL *smile at one another and rub legs
under the table.*

NICK. Fucking hippies.

Beat.

RACHEL. My mother keeps quietly hinting that we could cut
our shopping bills in half.

NICK. And that I should give up smoking.

AMY. I thought you had.

NICK. Yeah.

RACHEL. Cut out the drinking.

AMY. You're hardly drinking at all!

SIMON. Ah, but Nick's drinking for two.

> RACHEL *shoots a nervous glance at* SIMON.

NICK. It's none of her fucking business.

RACHEL. She thinks we're going to ask her to bail us out.

NICK. I'd rather plunge my testicles into a vat of acid.

AMY. Nick!

RACHEL. He's right. We can't ask her. She'd take over our lives.

SIMON. Is it really that bad?

NICK. Nah. It'll be fine. When I flog my *magnum opus*, the old cow'll be coming in her pantyhose.

AMY. Nick! Jesus.

RACHEL. We had the building society on. Bank wouldn't clear the mortgage.

AMY. That's bad, isn't it?

RACHEL. It's not great.

> *Pause.*

> Put it this way, it better not happen again in a hurry.

AMY. Lads, if there's anything we can do…

SIMON. How're you going to cover it this time?

NICK. We're going to beat the living shite out of Peter.

> SIMON *and* AMY *look momentarily puzzled.*

RACHEL. To pay Paul.

They get it.

Cash. From the credit card. But that's it then.

NICK. Nowhere to run.

Silence.

AMY. Well, I think you're amazing.

RACHEL. It's called denial.

She shivers.

Enough already! How's the exhibition?

AMY. Not bad. Up and down. You know… (*Apologetic.*) Pretty good, actually. Once we retrieved *The Dumb Waiter*, that is.

They all look puzzled.

Duncan Swift. Most hyped piece in the show, bloody huge… and the carriers managed to lose it somewhere between Runcorn and Watford. Twenty-four hours of pure terror. They found it in a depot eventually. In Hemel Hempstead. Mistaken for a consignment of beer glasses on its way to a CAMRA festival.

SIMON. That's modern art for you.

AMY. Excuse me! It's a nice piece of work!

RACHEL. A camera festival?

AMY. CAMRA! C-A-M-R-A.

NICK. Real ale, darling.

RACHEL. Yeuch.

NICK *and* SIMON *exchange meaningful nods.*

NICK. You ladies can't be expected to understand.

AMY. Oi, excuse me! Anyway, Simon wouldn't know a Dark Ruby from a pint of Ribena. (*To* NICK.) The only reason *you* know anything is cos you had to review one.

RACHEL (*to* NICK). A camra festival?

NICK. CAM-RA.

RACHEL. That's what I said.

She looks around. They're all trying to keep straight faces.

Uuuhh!

RACHEL *starts to laugh.*

So. You found the piece in a depot?

AMY (*nodding*). Such liars! Swore they'd delivered it, signature, everything. Then you ask them to prove it and lo and behold… Oh my God!

She flaps her arms in excitement.

(*To* NICK.) You know the January show?

NICK. Uh.

AMY. Remember Tristan?

NICK. Tristan… (*Remembering, suddenly interested.*) Oh, yeah?

AMY. He *gave* me one of the pieces!

NICK. You're kidding.

AMY. Afterwards. As a thank you. I totally forgot to say it to you.

NICK. Which one?

AMY. The doll. In the cabinet.

NICK. Jesus! What d'you do – fuck him?

AMY. You are such a prick. Come. I'll show you.

She drags him from the room.

Pause.

SIMON *puts on a mock-gloomy face.*

SIMON. She hasn't shown me yet.

RACHEL. That's because we're philistines.

SIMON. No, angel. *I* am a philistine. *You* are an artiste.

Beat.

RACHEL. I'm pregnant, Si.

Beat.

SIMON. Wahey!

RACHEL. Ssshhh!

SIMON. Oops. Sorry. You sly devil! That's wonderful news!

Beat.

Isn't it?

She smiles, hesitantly, and nods.

SIMON *leaps up and gives her a big hug – he's genuinely delighted.*

Aw!

He sits back down, pulling his chair closer to hers.

Not said anything to Ames yet, then? Ooh. She's not going to like that! I love being the first to know things! Don't worry, mum's the word! (*He realises the joke.*) Mum's the word!

RACHEL. I've not told Nick.

Long pause.

SIMON. Ah.

RACHEL. I… It couldn't be a more difficult time.

SIMON. No.

Silence.

RACHEL. What if he doesn't want it, Simon?

SIMON. Oh… I think…

RACHEL. Now, I mean. In the circumstances.

Beat.

Or, I don't know. What's worse? That he assumes it's going to be like the rest? That he doesn't need to worry because it's not going to…

Their eyes meet.

SIMON. Yes. No.

RACHEL. We'd stopped trying.

Pause.

Decided. It must have been, literally… as I was conceiving. That's it. Can't keep going through it all. Enough.

Beat.

And Nick was so relieved. He was so relieved.

She looks SIMON *in the eye. Her excitement is becoming evident.*

The thing is, Si… I knew. Almost straightaway, after that conversation. That's never happened to me before. You hear of it happening. To lots of people. But never to me. So strong. This feeling. A… warmth. A pulse… It's different this time, I know it. I feel different.

Pause.

It's possible Amy may have guessed.

SIMON. Hmm. A fiendish intuition, that girl.

Beat.

I don't mean to be indelicate, lovely, but… how long…?

RACHEL. Seven weeks. Early days.

Pause.

SIMON. And Nicholas? Definitely no inkling?

RACHEL. Oh, you know Nick. He kind of waits to be told. In a good way.

Beat.

And we've been… giving each other a bit of space recently, so…

SIMON. Uh-huh. Yes. Yes, I see.

Pause.

Well. I'm no expert, angel… but my gut instinct is that you're going to have to tell him.

Beat.

I'm sure it'll be all right. Truly.

RACHEL. We're about to lose the house.

SIMON. Then maybe he needs to bite the bullet. Put the book on hold? Proper job and so on.

RACHEL. I can't ask him to do that. Not now.

Beat.

Do you think Amy will say anything?

SIMON. Oh, most unlikely, I would have thought. Discretion of a mule. Hard to countenance, but it's true. She tells me nothing.

The others are heard approaching.

RACHEL. It's just they…

SIMON. D'you want me to talk to him?

RACHEL. No. Thanks. I'll… find a time.

AMY and NICK burst noisily back into the room. NICK is tearing at his hair.

NICK. AAAAR! It's not fucking fair!! My life is crap.

Beat.

SIMON pushes back his chair. AMY gives him a quizzical look.

RACHEL (*laughing*). And I love you too.

NICK. Oh. Baby.

He crosses to give her a hug. She glances briefly at SIMON *over* NICK*'s shoulder.*

Not crap. Just… (*He starts to laugh.*) different…

RACHEL *thumps him and they break apart, both laughing.*

Suddenly AMY *freezes and signals for quiet. They all stop to listen.*

SIMON (*groaning*). Noooo.

There is the sound of a child crying upstairs.

(*Pointing at* AMY.) That was you. And your doll in a cabinet.

AMY. Not my turn, kiddo.

Pause.

I did the last time. *And* the time before that, in fact.

SIMON. Well, send your arty friend, then.

NICK. Me? You have to be fucking kidding. You want it to survive the night, yeah?

SIMON *glances nervously at* RACHEL. AMY *follows his gaze.*

RACHEL *is looking at* NICK.

An uneasy silence.

RACHEL *stands.*

RACHEL. I'll go.

She leaves the room.

Silence.

The child cries again. AMY *looks meaningfully at* SIMON.

SIMON. Oh, all right. But you owe me big time, lady.

He pauses to kiss her forehead as he leaves the room.

Pause.

AMY (*angrily*). *You*. Have got to get your act together.

NICK (*innocent*). What?

AMY. 'You want it to survive the night'? What kind of a question is that?

NICK. It was a joke.

AMY. What are you planning to do with your own kids when they come along? Lock them in a cupboard for the night?

Beat.

NICK. It's not going to happen.

AMY. You don't know that.

NICK. Oh, come off it! You and I both know it.

Pause.

Anyway, we've given up trying.

AMY. Really?

NICK. Really. Jesus. What's the big deal? It was a joke.

AMY. How's Rachel about that?

NICK. She's fine. She was... I dunno... relieved.

AMY. Nick.

NICK. Fuck it, Amy! We can't keep pretending each time that everything's going to be all right. It isn't going to happen. There's something wrong. With her... bits.

AMY. Her 'bits'? Her 'bits'! How old are you? Honestly, you should be strung up by the bollocks.

NICK *sighs*.

Nick, you *have* to be more supportive.

Pause.

I know it doesn't come easy...

He smiles.

Poor girl. What if she did get pregnant again? Accidentally.

NICK. She won't.

AMY. What then?

NICK. We can't go through another one.

AMY. But if…

NICK. Christ, Ames, just leave it, will you!

Beat.

She hasn't been near me in weeks.

Pause.

AMY. I'm sorry.

She stretches out her hand and takes his.

NICK. That's okay. Inevitable.

AMY. I wasn't… I just… Well, sometimes I think there's quite a lot to be said for pretending.

NICK. Lying, you mean.

AMY. No!

NICK. Rachel's congenitally incapable of it. That's what I love about her.

Pause.

AMY *withdraws her hand.*

AMY. Oh well, who knows? Things could still work out, couldn't they. After a bit of a break. It's not unheard of.

NICK. Stop! Amy. Please.

Beat.

Anyhow, we can't afford a sodding baby!

AMY *stares at him.*

Oh… piss. I do love her, Ames. I love her so much.

AMY. I know you do.

Beat.

They look at each other.

NICK. I would never do anything to hurt her.

Sound of a door opening upstairs.

Pause.

AMY (*raising her voice slightly*). Remember Toby Mercier?

NICK. Froggy.

AMY. Bumped into him the other day. At an opening.

Pause.

Bald as a bald thing.

NICK. Ha!

RACHEL *enters.*

AMY. Apart from that, hasn't changed a bit.

NICK. What's he up to?

He holds his arms out for RACHEL *who sits on his knee. He kisses her.*

AMY. Well… As far as I could tell, he's to and fro to the Continent, picking up as much as he can fit inside his coat, carting it all back and flogging it wherever he can.

NICK *snorts contemptuously.*

So far I think the only thing he's sold for more than fifty quid is some obscure little Rodin he picked up in a backstreet in Verona. That *was* in Christie's, mind you.

RACHEL. A Rodin?

AMY. There are a *lot* of sketches…

Pause.

RACHEL. How does he survive?

NICK (*squeezing her*). He's dead, baby.

RACHEL (*laughing*). Fool! What's-his-name. Your friend.

AMY. Private income.

NICK. Bastard.

AMY (*to* RACHEL). That was always the way. Even at college. It used to drive Nick insane with jealousy.

NICK. I'm a more balanced person now.

SIMON *enters.*

SIMON. Personally, I've always found you to be on a very even keel…

NICK. Watch your mouth, *Dad*.

SIMON. Who are you calling 'Dad'…

RACHEL *freezes.* AMY *rises abruptly, almost knocking over her chair.* SIMON *realises his near-mistake.* NICK *remains oblivious.*

AMY. Right! Coffee, anyone?

SIMON *moves hastily towards a cupboard.*

SIMON. We have petits fours!

RACHEL. You do not!

NICK. You posh fuckers.

Blackout.

Scene Two

The same table, the same kitchen. Five weeks later.

The mood is one of shock. RACHEL *and* AMY *are alone. A bottle lies broken on the floor, red wine mingled with broken glass.* RACHEL *sits motionless, as if she's seen a ghost.*

Slowly, AMY *sets the table with a half-eaten main course, a thus-far-untouched cheeseboard and a couple of near-empty wine bottles, along with a bottle of port and half a bottle of brandy. She moves around the broken glass on the floor, appearing not to see it.*

RACHEL *looks up. Briefly their eyes meet.* RACHEL *averts her gaze.*

AMY *bends to sweep the glass into a dustpan. She deposits it in a newspaper, and wraps it up. As she does so, she flinches and puts her finger to her mouth.*

She puts the rolled-up newspaper in the bin, picks up a glass of wine and leans against the work surface.

She watches RACHEL *carefully.*

Silence.

RACHEL. Do you think they'll come back?

AMY. Si will talk to him.

Pause.

It's what he's best at.

Beat.

RACHEL. I should have told him. Weeks ago.

AMY. So? He's like a kid. His pride is hurt, that's all. He used to do this kind of thing all the time in the old days.

RACHEL *looks at her.*

He'll get over it. Trust me.

Silence.

RACHEL. What the hell possessed me? I just… I kept thinking things would get better. I don't know. That we might have some kind of a… (*She laughs wryly.*) breakthrough…

Beat.

You're bleeding.

AMY *looks in surprise at her finger. Blood runs down on to her hand.*

AMY. Shit.

She reaches for a roll of kitchen towel.

RACHEL. I'm sorry, Amy.

AMY. I'll live.

Pause.

RACHEL. I mean, partly I thought, you know, if I could get through the first bit, then at least… at least he'd be spared that. And then… Oh God.

Pause.

He's not coming back, is he?

AMY. Rachel! Stop. Of course he is.

RACHEL. I was so happy! After today. And here, with you two. I actually thought it might help. Having you there. That he might take it better. That it might be… easier.

Beat.

It was sneaky.

AMY. Come on, Rach… You have to stop beating yourself up.

RACHEL. *I* was sneaky.

AMY. It's not your fault.

RACHEL *looks at her.*

Beat.

It will be all right.

RACHEL. Oh, Ames, it's so *unfair*! Money! As if we didn't
have enough to worry about! Such a stupid, petty thing. Half
the time it feels as though we should just be able to carry on
indefinitely. Everyone else seems to be. It feels enormous
and utterly insignificant all at once… You know, a hundred
years ago, we'd probably have been okay. Fifty even. And
now suddenly I'm feeling like a failure for not being able to
juggle ten credit cards.

AMY *has been watching her closely.*

AMY. You're certainly not alone, there.

RACHEL. But surely something's got to give, hasn't it? I mean,
I'm not really imagining we can keep shoring it up for ever.
And what then? We're out on our own, Nick and I. We're not
property tycoons. We have no fallback. No 'mansion' in
Hackney, no little gold mine in the sun. But we're not poor
either. And if we claimed to be, we'd quite rightly be
laughed out of town. We have debt. We owe a lot of money.
But we're middle class, whatever that means. And we have
well-off parents.

She looks anxiously at the door.

Pause.

I'm sorry. I wasn't brought up to be in debt.

AMY (*smiling*). But you were brought up in a manner to which
you've become accustomed.

RACHEL *laughs dryly.*

Have you actually sat down together and talked about it? The
money thing. About what you're going to do?

RACHEL. He won't. You know what he's like.

Pause.

We defaulted. Properly this time. I've been on to them every day for a week now, trying to sort it out... And still, all he does is joke. Convincing himself that the solution is just going be handed to us on a plate.

AMY *looks thoughtful.*

AMY. Nick's approach to life has always been selective.

RACHEL. To be fair, it's no wonder, really... that he's running. This... all of it... it's terrible timing for him. The worst. Right when he finally seems to be getting somewhere.

AMY. Ha! Don't fall into that trap, whatever you do. Not when it could just as easily take him another ten years.

Beat.

Look. I've known Nick a long time now. And I can categorically vouch for the fact that he *always* seems finally to be getting somewhere when the time's about to run out. It's the way he is. It's a defence mechanism.

Pause.

This way he's not to blame if he fails.

Beat.

RACHEL. So, who is?

Silence.

(*Rising.*) I have to look for him.

Sounds of male voices approaching. The front door opens. RACHEL *and* AMY *look at one another.* RACHEL *sits abruptly.* NICK *appears, framed in the doorway with* SIMON *at his shoulder.*

Pause.

Hello.

He crosses to her in silence, kneels and embraces her, burying his face in her lap. She puts her hands in his hair and bends to kiss his head.

SIMON. Hormones.

SIMON crosses to his seat.

You may call me Wise One. Oh Great Healer. He Who Must Be Obeyed.

He peers at the cheese.

Ah. The Gift. Most generous indeed.

He sniffs it.

No knives? Excellent precaution.

They laugh.

AMY gets up and goes looking for a knife.

AMY. We thought you might rend it asunder with your mind powers.

NICK raises his head from RACHEL's lap. He looks at her, then kisses her tummy.

RACHEL. I'm so sorry.

AMY *(to* SIMON*)*. What have you done with everything?

AMY looks in the dishwasher.

NICK. Did you get a picture?

RACHEL rises and goes to her handbag. She produces a scan picture which she brings back to the table. She gives it to NICK, who is back in his own seat. He stares at it in silence.

AMY brings a large carving knife to the table. She pauses at NICK's shoulder to look at the photo.

AMY. Wow.

NICK turns to RACHEL and smiles. Hesitantly, she returns the smile.

SIMON. May I?

NICK passes the photo to SIMON, who looks at it and chuckles.

Silence as they all look at the picture.

AMY *breaks away and hands the knife to* SIMON, *who contemplates it in mild surprise before handing the photo back to* NICK *and returning his attention to the cheese.*

Marvellous!

(*Indicating the cheeses.*) So what are these?

Beat.

RACHEL (*dragging her eyes away from* NICK *and the photo*). Um… well, we're not entirely sure. We found this funny little place, just off the Broadway… Looks as though it's been there for ever…

NICK *puts the photo down in the middle of the table.*

SIMON. Ah.

NICK (*spooky voice*)….But neither of us has ever seen it before…

RACHEL. We think he's Italian.

NICK. Remember Mr Benn?

SIMON. Mmn. You journeyed to Italian land, yes?

RACHEL. This one's like a cross between Parmesan and something sweeter… and kind of… sheepier.

AMY. Interesting.

SIMON. Sheepy cheese. My favourite.

NICK. It has a certain palate-stripper quality. Pleasure-pain. Right up your alley.

SIMON. I don't know what you're implying, sir.

AMY (*poking one of the other cheeses with a dirty fork*). And what about that one?

RACHEL. That's just French.

AMY. Oh.

SIMON. Well. No contest. It's sheepy palate-stripper for me.

He cuts a substantial slice and pops it into his mouth.

Ouf!

RACHEL. Oh, it's very strong…

AMY reaches over. SIMON attempts to stop her but she cuts herself a large slice and puts it in her mouth.

…and really salty!

AMY. Shit!

SIMON. Ooh dear.

AMY grimaces and spits it out into her hand. SIMON rushes to the tap and fills a glass of water which AMY gulps down.

Amy's rather sensitive when it comes to seasoning, aren't you, lover?

Beat.

A creature of myth. Like the Princess and the Pea.

RACHEL. You don't like salt?

AMY goes to the sink, spits water into it and refills the glass.

SIMON. Upbringing.

AMY. Oh, for goodness' sake, Simon.

She swills water round her mouth.

SIMON. Grandparents. On a tight budget. A tad too much in the diet. We have tried to help.

He looks at NICK, who nods.

AMY (*spitting*). What, with your stupid experiment?

SIMON. Actually, I meant in terms of distilling your palate… But I'll have you know that 'stupid experiment' was conducted in full accordance with the principles of scientific inquiry.

AMY. You were bladdered, Simon.

RACHEL. What experiment?

They look at AMY.

AMY. Uh! This dumb thing that they *still* go on about like they were present at the first moon landing or something.

Beat.

There was an article, that Nick got commissioned to write. Maybe six months after Simon and I first got together? About salt.

SIMON. 'The Essential Commodity.' Salt as currency. Salt in the body. Preserving qualities, etcetera, etcetera... Bloody fascinating stuff.

AMY. And although these two had already met lots of times – obviously – I think you could say that, up to then, they'd been kind of... doggy with one another...

NICK. 'Doggy'? What the...?

AMY. Territorial. 'I've wee'd here and it's mine.'

NICK. Cobblers.

RACHEL *looks at* NICK, *who doesn't return her gaze.*

AMY. You were a nightmare, the pair of you!

She turns back to RACHEL.

Anyway, finally, one fateful night, they hit upon... an activity which seemed to... enthuse them.

SIMON. Old Nick had got a bee in his bonnet...

NICK *gives a derisory snort.*

...about what makes something too salty or not salty enough or just right...

Beat.

RACHEL. That's a taste thing. Surely?

SIMON. Ah! Up to a point, yes. But Nick's notion… was that there was an absolute – like absolute zero – where the change happened. Genius.

AMY. A grain that tips the scale.

SIMON. But *which* grain?

AMY. So… they got hideously drunk and stayed up for twenty-four hours counting out individual grains of salt, adding them one by one to a pan of… some kind of soup, I think…

NICK. Vichyssoise.

AMY. And tasting it every time – in between shots of tequila – until they fell over. Thereby resolving…

SIMON *gives* RACHEL *a wink*.

SIMON. Absolutely zero!

NICK. *Quod erat demonstrandum*.

SIMON. And we've kind of rubbed along together ever since. Haven't we, me ol' mucker?

RACHEL (*to* NICK). You never told me about that.

NICK (*not meeting* RACHEL*'s gaze*). I'd chosen to erase it from my memory.

SIMON. Ames was terribly disapproving. I think she liked it better when we didn't get on.

AMY. I just don't see that twenty-four hours of being off your heads is necessarily something to be celebrated, that's all.

NICK. Don't knock it till you try it.

SIMON. Anyway, it was more than mere inebriation. I'd say it had a touch of the transcendentals about it…

NICK *nods*.

AMY. Oh God.

SIMON. Exactly! By three in the morning, one had definitely… crossed a line, so to speak. Entered a new spiritual dimension.

AMY. Ha!

SIMON. What?

AMY. Simon, you're about as spiritual as a wombat. (*Indicating the cheeseboard.*) I don't think I dare risk any more of that, I'm afraid.

RACHEL. Oh…! I forgot!

RACHEL leaps to her feet, goes to her bag and begins to rummage.

We found new biscuits too…

NICK pulls a face.

Kind of like… savoury wafers.

Pause.

SIMON. Yum.

RACHEL. They're quite nice.

She produces the packet and raises her head, just as NICK is miming vomiting under the table. He gives her a cheeky grin.

Oh, Nick. Please don't.

AMY. You okay?

RACHEL (*moving to sit*). Uf. Yeah. Eaten too much, maybe. Just a bit… bloated.

SIMON. *Loving* this sheepy cheese, ladies.

RACHEL (*laughing weakly*). Sorry, Si. Oh. Oh dear.

AMY. Oh, sweetie.

RACHEL. No! Don't be nice to me, for God's sake!

AMY laughs.

NICK (*putting his arm round her*). Babe. Aw. It'll be all right. Honest.

RACHEL. Ha.

NICK. Earlier. I was just… I don't know. I felt…

SIMON. Expendable?

AMY. Simon.

SIMON. Sorry.

NICK. A bit sad.

SIMON *picks up dishes from the table, carries them to the sink and begins to unload and load the dishwasher.*

RACHEL (*starting to cry*). Oh God.

Beat.

I thought you'd gone.

NICK. It's okay. Ssshhh. It's okay.

AMY *shoots him a look and begins to gather up dishes.*

It's just…

Pause.

Well, I have feelings too, you know.

A strangled noise from AMY.

RACHEL *and* NICK *hug.*

Long pause.

RACHEL (*to* SIMON *and* AMY). I'm sorry, you two. To land all this on you.

SIMON. Think nothing of it.

Beat.

That's what Amy's here for.

AMY. Simon's here for the cheese.

SIMON *grins.*

They laugh.

RACHEL. Why does everything have to be so hard? I know I'm not allowed to say that. But it is.

NICK. We'll work it out.

NICK rises and starts busying himself with the biscuits – fetching a plate, removing them from the packet, arranging them.

RACHEL. Will we?

Pause.

How will we?

An uneasy silence.

(*Rising.*) I'm sorry. I think I need to lie down.

AMY. Use our room. You want water?

RACHEL *nods.*

NICK. I'll bring it.

RACHEL *leaves.*

Pause.

The sound of a door closing upstairs.

AMY. You okay?

NICK nods. He goes to a cupboard, fetches a tumbler and fills it from the tap. He looks at them.

NICK. She's right. It's too hard.

Beat.

Bollocks.

He turns to leave.

AMY. Nick!

She looks at SIMON.

Simon and I... We've been talking and... well, we wanted...

Beat.

We've got something we wanted to run by you. Nothing to worry about and... certainly not something you need to make a decision on now. Just a proposal... for the two of you to discuss.

Beat.

Kind of like...

SIMON. An offer.

AMY. Yes. Yes, an offer of help. A gift.

NICK *looks at* SIMON, *who nods.*

Pause.

No strings.

Blackout.

Scene Three

The same kitchen. Eight weeks later.

AMY *is absent.*

There is a party atmosphere. The music is loud. RACHEL *is now obviously pregnant.*

NICK *is cooking. He is flamboyant and clearly skilled. He takes his ingredients from a couple of carrier bags placed beside him on the work surface, rinses, chops and throws them into a pan at top speed. A jar of salt lies open beside him.* RACHEL *fills a small bowl from it.* NICK *is liberal with his seasoning of the food, scattering salt across the work surface.* RACHEL *picks some up, throwing it over* NICK's *left shoulder, and then her own.*

She is setting the table in preparation for a main course. She places the salt on the table along with a loaf of bread, some olive oil, balsamic vinegar, a couple of half-empty bowls of olives, a large jug of water, four plates, four wine glasses, cutlery and three dirty side plates. The fourth side plate has an untouched starter on it – a couple of pinchos. Occasionally RACHEL *hesitates. She knows where some things are but not others.*

SIMON *is doing silly dancing, of which he is the master. As he dances, he opens two bottles of wine and places them on the table, along with an empty bottle and a half-full one.*

In the midst of this, AMY *enters, breathless, dressed in a stylish suit.* SIMON *gives her a look – 'What time do you call this?' She hugs* RACHEL, *kisses* NICK, *dumps her handbag and keys on a work surface and removes her jacket. She and* SIMON *exchange a peck on the lips and a few words. She leaves the room, picking up one of the pinchos from her plate as she does so.*

SIMON *fetches a bottle of champagne from the fridge and champagne flutes from a cupboard. He attempts to open the bottle.* NICK *and* RACHEL *duck.*

The cork pops. They cheer and whoop as SIMON *pours the champagne with a flourish.* AMY *rushes in clutching a bundle of clothes which she starts shoving into the washing machine.*

AMY (*to* SIMON). Did you bath Rosie?

As SIMON *pours the fourth glass,* RACHEL *makes as if to stop him.*

SIMON. You bloody well will, missus!

AMY. Oh, one glass won't hurt, Rach. Honest. With Sam I drank right the way through.

SIMON (*nodding in agreement*). Copious amounts.

AMY (*to* SIMON). Thank you. (*To* RACHEL.) And he's turned out all right. In spite of his father.

RACHEL *smiles.*

(*To* SIMON.) She appears to be covered in –

SIMON. Black marker. I know. *Mea culpa.* Come along, people!

He hands a glass to RACHEL *and then* AMY.

AMY. So why is she green?

SIMON. That's what happens when you try and scrub it off.

He indicates NICK, *who is in his own world.*

Ooh, look at him go! The boy's inspired!

NICK *scrapes the final ingredients into the pan with a flourish and stirs them vigorously as the others look on in admiration.*

RACHEL (*laughing*). He is! He's on a roll.

Pause.

Has he told you there's been some interest? In the book.

SIMON. He did mutter something. About a friend of Dan's?

RACHEL. Yeah. It's a big agency, apparently.

SIMON. Aha!

RACHEL. And they're really enthusiastic.

AMY. Wow.

SIMON. *Excellente!* Doesn't surprise me in the slightest.

AMY. You mean he might actually do it?

RACHEL. He's got till the beginning of December, I think, to get a full draft to them.

SIMON. Calls for a drink, I would say. Nicol-arse!

He waves a dripping glass in NICK*'s direction.*

Thy cup overfloweth!

With a final stir of the pan, NICK *comes over to take the glass.*

He's wearing an apron, clearly not his.

SIMON *looks him up and down.*

Very nice.

He pats him on the bottom. NICK *slaps his hand away.*

SIMON *raises his glass.*

Now. Unaccustomed as I am…

AMY. Oh Christ.

SIMON (*to* AMY). Thank you, dear… (*Turning to* NICK *and* RACHEL.) I would simply like to express to our beloved friends, how truly happy it makes us to see you thriving… And producing, no less! Many, many congratulations on your… exploits to date…

AMY. Speak English, Simon!

He glances at her crossly.

SIMON. …and may you continue to prosper and flourish and expound and… progenise… and…

AMY. It's wonderful! All of it. And we're delighted to be part of it and to have been able to help!

Beat.

Aw. Look at the two of you! Who says money can't buy happiness, eh?

SIMON. Good God. Steady on, old girl.

AMY *raises her glass.*

AMY. To Nick and Rachel!

SIMON. Rachel and Nick!

Laughing, they clink glasses and drink.

And may I add, lovely, how well your condition becomes you!

AMY. It's not a disease, Simon.

SIMON (*ignoring her*). You look radiant, my dear.

RACHEL *smiles her thanks.*

NICK. Hoorah!

RACHEL (*to* NICK). You sounded like Simon then.

NICK looks mildly irritated.

SIMON. Do I smell burning?

NICK. Bugger.

He rushes back to the cooker and stirs the contents of the pan vigorously.

RACHEL *and* AMY *sit.*

AMY (*to* RACHEL). So? How do you feel?

Pause.

RACHEL. Ooh.

She places her palms face down on the table.

Weird.

Beat.

It's like that thing – standing on the edge of a cliff and being so scared of falling that I almost think I'm going to jump in spite of myself. That I'm going to do something, choose to do something, that'll cause it all to end.

SIMON. Everything in the balance, eh?

AMY gives him a look.

What? Uncharted waters and all that.

RACHEL. Well, you can't just not think about it… Obviously. About what's… gone before. Ten weeks and three days. Sixteen weeks and a day. Nineteen weeks… Each time, each time fighting the urge to stay home, lock the doors, bar the windows.

Beat.

And now. What am I supposed to do with now? Stop breathing?

AMY. But it must mean something. To get to this point. Haven't they said that?

RACHEL. They've said it's a good sign.

NICK. They've been incredibly positive.

RACHEL. They have.

To AMY *and* SIMON.

They have.

She laughs.

But who's to say it's not negativity keeping this pregnancy going!

NICK. I think you could afford to let go a little.

RACHEL. Yes.

Beat.

So did Nick tell you we had the second scan?

AMY. Oh my God, no! Is everything…? (*Gasps.*) Do you know the sex?

NICK. I wasn't allowed to ask.

RACHEL. It's all fine. That's not true. It's just it would've been difficult – you knowing and me not.

NICK. It's okay. I've come to terms with the fact that we're not going to agree on anything just now.

RACHEL. Stop. We do agree on things.

SIMON. Personally, I think you're remarkably amicable.

Beat.

Given what Rachel has to put up with.

AMY *thumps him.*

RACHEL. Thank you, Simon.

AMY. Well, you're bound to have your ups and downs, aren't you?

She looks intently from one to the other.

RACHEL. We're fine. It's all fine.

NICK. Right, plates please, ladies and gents!

AMY. Me! Me, me!

She picks up the plates from the table and carries them over.

It smells amazing.

SIMON. Ah, he's a whore in the kitchen.

NICK *grabs a brown-paper bag full of leaves and chucks it to* AMY, *who empties them into a bowl.*

He ladles what looks like a type of paella onto the four plates.

They carry everything to the table. NICK *puts his own plate down first, then hands one to* SIMON.

They sit.

SIMON *raises his glass again.*

AMY. Oh, here we go.

RACHEL (*laughing*). Oh, poor Simon. You've really got it in for him tonight!

SIMON (*to* RACHEL). Thank you, angel. I've married a harridan. I have a fishwife for a spouse.

NICK *raises his glass.*

NICK. Cheers!

SIMON. *Salud*!

AMY. *Gesundheit.*

They clink.

NICK. Right. Tuck in.

They eat.

There is silence for a while.

AMY (*with her mouth full*). Nick, this is incredible!

SIMON. You've excelled yourself, old boy! Creative genius –
never let them tell you otherwise.

Pause.

Now then. What's that extra… bit of heat I'm experiencing?

RACHEL. I'm not sure we want to know!

SIMON *gives her a wink.*

AMY. It's called chilli powder, Simon.

SIMON (*horrified*). No, no, no! Nothing so mundane.

Pause.

NICK *and* SIMON *eye one another competitively. At last,*
SIMON *shakes his head.*

SIMON. Habanero?

NICK. Scotch bonnet.

SIMON. Aargh!

AMY. Scotch what?

RACHEL (*laughing*). Bonnet. It's in the shape of a little
tam-o'-shanter…

AMY. A kind of chilli?

NICK. Yep.

AMY (*to* SIMON). So I was right.

NICK. Light years from your ordinary common-or-garden
chilli, though…

SIMON (*to* AMY). Ha!

RACHEL (*rubbing her tummy*). I love it! (*To* AMY.) You keep
it whole and just pop it on the top. Right at the end of the
cooking, so the flavour's quite subtle… (*To* NICK *and*
SIMON.) But it's actually one of the hottest in the world,
isn't it?

NICK. Hotter than a jalapeño. Hundred thousand units. Maybe more.

SIMON. That baby's going to be one tough cookie.

AMY. What do you mean, 'units'?

SIMON. On the Scoville scale.

AMY. Get lost.

SIMON. What?

AMY. There's no such thing.

SIMON. Oh yes there is. American chap. Wilbur, I believe. Measured the piquancy of chillis.

AMY looks around for support. NICK nods.

NICK. Amount of capsaicin. Stimulating the nerve endings.

SIMON gives a shudder of pleasure.

SIMON. Ooh, there's nothing quite like it.

NICK. Google him if you don't believe us.

AMY *(to* SIMON). How do you know these things?

Beat.

Bloody public school.

NICK *(irritated)*. Hardly. It's science. Food is just science.

Pause.

AMY. Well, I can't taste the difference.

SIMON shies away from her in mock-horror.

SIMON. Aaagh!

AMY looks annoyed. She pokes her food irritably.

AMY. So what are these then, Einstein? I don't know what these are either.

NICK. Which?

SIMON. Oh yes! (*Raking through his rice with a fork.*) I wondered about those, actually! A hitherto undiscovered crustacean… Oh. (*Disappointed.*) I appear to have eaten all mine.

AMY. They're shellfish, aren't they? I thought Rachel couldn't eat shellfish?

NICK *looks up abruptly.*

RACHEL. Oh, that's okay.

SIMON. I was searching for a name.

RACHEL. I think that's just being overcautious, really…

SIMON. The mobster!

RACHEL. Anyway, there's plenty of chicken.

SIMON. No. Too big.

Beat.

RACHEL. And, of course, I have Simon.

She proffers her plate, indicating a small pile of seafood to one side of it.

SIMON. Ah! Angel.

NICK *takes a large swig of wine, draining his glass, and watching as* RACHEL *transfers the seafood to* SIMON's *plate.*

The crimp! The shrollop?

NICK. You should have said something.

SIMON *pierces one with his fork and holds it up admiringly.*

SIMON. No, not glamorous enough for you, my lovely!

RACHEL. It doesn't matter. Nick… honestly.

NICK *shakes his head in irritation, grabs an opened bottle and sloshes red wine abruptly into each of the glasses, including* RACHEL's, *spilling a pool of it onto the table in the process.*

AMY (*quickly, referring to the wine*). Different… Never mind. Too late.

NICK glances at the label before replacing the bottle on the table and raising his glass.

NICK. A toast!

AMY. Another one?

SIMON. Good Lord!

They pick up their glasses in surprise. Wine drips from the table. RACHEL attempts to stem the flow with her spare hand, ending up with wine running from her arm.

NICK. To Amy and Simon! For an Act of Pure Genius – I mean, Generosity.

SIMON. Oh… Piffle.

RACHEL. Simon and Amy. Thank you… From the bottom of our hearts.

AMY. Uh-uh. I'm sorry. I can't drink to myself… And I can't not drink. (*She raises her glass.*) To friendship!

SIMON. Friendship!

They drink.

NICK. And undiscovered talent!

SIMON. Hoorah…!

They drink.

SIMON raises his glass.

AMY. And knowing when to stop?

He lowers it, grinning.

SIMON. Talking of which, I took a look at the manuscript, by the way.

NICK is suddenly alert.

NICK. Oh. Great. I assumed…

SIMON. Well, I've only skimmed it so far.

Pause.

It's good, though. Yes. Definitely. Good job, old chap.

Pause.

Maybe we could find a quiet moment. Have a chat about it. Later on, perhaps.

NICK. Right.

Silence.

NICK *watches as* SIMON *sprinkles salt liberally on the remainder of his food.*

AMY. Anyway. Things are looking up.

RACHEL. Oh, you wouldn't believe the difference! Honestly. We cannot thank you enough... God. Nick even braved the bank with me! Didn't you, my love?

AMY. Well, as we said... it's not like it's a big thing. The money was there and this seemed like the most sensible use for it, that's all...

SIMON. And not a loan.

AMY. Not a loan.

RACHEL. No.

Pause.

It's ridiculous, really. When you think about it. The turnaround. I mean, suddenly, we're seeing all these poor people on the news, queuing around the block... panicking about their savings and... Well, I'm not naive... I do know it probably won't last, but just for once, it seems that... we're kind of fine... and it's the rest of the world that's in crisis...

SIMON. Reversal of fortune...

RACHEL. We've never even *had* any savings!

SIMON. Couldn't be better.

NICK *is watching* RACHEL *carefully.*

RACHEL. Yes. I don't know. I mean, it's amazing. It really is. The relief! Not living under that cloud. Not fighting every time over who's not going to answer the phone…

Pause.

And it was so generous of you. So generous.

AMY *looks from* NICK *to* RACHEL.

AMY. But…?

Beat.

RACHEL (*laughing*). No buts… Not really…

She glances at NICK.

I did have a little wobble. At the beginning.

Beat.

But we pretty much got over it.

Pause.

It's just… well –

NICK. Oh Christ. Here we go.

RACHEL. What about if you *did* need it back…

SIMON. We won't.

RACHEL. …at some point?

SIMON. We invest in the right commodity, lovely.

RACHEL. But what if…?

SIMON. No worries on that score. Next?

Beat.

AMY. Look, Rach, we thought really hard about what to do with that money… Simon and his father, they don't exactly… speak…

SIMON. Because he's an avaricious old cunt.

AMY. He is an avaricious old cunt...

SIMON. Trying to dodge the tax man. Trying to cheat fate by clinging to life for another seven emphysemic years so he can put the rest of us through more hell.

AMY. So he's passing on his assets.

SIMON. Ha!

AMY. Anyway, this is what we decided.

SIMON. It was you two or Save the Children.

Beat.

Joke.

AMY. Don't worry, it's not like we're giving you all of it. There's plenty more where that came from.

SIMON *sighs and puts his head on his hands.*

Pause.

RACHEL. Wow.

NICK. Happy?

RACHEL. Yes.

Beat.

(*Laughing.*) Kind of.

Beat.

It's just, oh, I don't know... I somehow feel we should be fending for ourselves, that's all. You know. 'You're not using it, so why should we?' 'There are so many people more desperate than us...'

Beat.

It feels a bit easy. As if we've not really done anything to deserve it...

AMY. Of course you have.

Beat.

We love you.

NICK. They love us.

SIMON. We do. Truly, madly, deeply.

AMY. Rachel. It's a gift.

Beat.

We wanted to give it to you. We felt good about giving it to you.

RACHEL. And don't get me wrong, it's so kind of you…

NICK. We'd do it for them. We said that.

RACHEL. Ye-es.

AMY. We know you would.

RACHEL. Given half a chance.

NICK. Fuck it, just leave it, will you, Rach?

Pause.

SIMON. Look, I tell you what. An idea.

Beat.

If it helps… why not think of it as a commission?

AMY. Yes! Nick can finish the book. It'll take some of the pressure off with… (*She indicates* RACHEL*'s tummy.*) everything. And then afterwards… after the baby's born… Well, you might even be able to go back to the orchestra at some point, mightn't you, or at least, I don't know – how does it work?

RACHEL (*laughing*). You have to practise. A lot. It might be a while, I think! (*She inspects her hands.*) The bizarre thing is they actually feel better. Better than they have in years. Pregnancy's usually something that brings it on.

AMY. A friend of mine had chronic sciatica for years until she got pregnant. Within a fortnight of her finding out, whoosh! Gone.

SIMON (*to* AMY). I hesitate to bring it up, oh love of my life, but somewhat closer to the action, no?

RACHEL (*laughing*). What is? A bottom?

AMY (*to* SIMON). Why can't you just say what you mean?

NICK (*interrupting loudly*). Anyway, we're not going to fall out over it.

He looks at RACHEL. AMY *follows his gaze.*

Beat.

AMY. I presume he means the money.

SIMON. Ah, yes. I'm sure we're big enough and ugly enough to cope.

AMY *opens her mouth to speak.*

(*Pointing at her.*) Don't even think about it.

Suspended beat.

NICK. Salad.

AMY. Mmm. Yes, please. Fingers?

NICK. Unfortunately, no.

AMY *slaps him playfully across the head. He hands her the salad bowl and she helps herself, passing it on to* SIMON, *who does likewise and passes it to* RACHEL.

Of course, there is an operation you can have.

SIMON *and* AMY *simultaneously pick a leaf from their plates and pop it into their mouths.*

But Rach doesn't buy in to modern medicine, do you, my sweet?

AMY. Wow!

SIMON. Pokey!

AMY. What is that?

RACHEL. Umbrian rocket. Different, isn't it?

AMY. Amazing. (*Turning to* RACHEL.) Sorry. They can
operate?

SIMON. You're on a bit of an Italian... thingy, just now, aren't
you.

AMY. Apart from the paella, you mean.

SIMON. Well, they've got their little shop... We haven't got
anything like that. Except for those damned designer hippies
opposite the Tube, who means test you before they let you in
the door.

NICK. That's because you're from the right side of the tracks,
mate.

*He rises abruptly to fetch another bottle of wine and a
corkscrew from the work surface.*

Just slumming it for the evening with the hoi polloi. Some of
us have to make the best of it.

RACHEL. It's called a 'release' – which is rather lovely –
because it takes the pressure off the nerve.

NICK. Bingo.

He uncorks the bottle.

RACHEL. But when it comes down to it, it means opening up
the wrist, across here... and cutting through the ligament.

AMY. Ugh.

RACHEL. Exactly!

NICK. It's a minor operation.

RACHEL. It just doesn't seem right to me. I can't help feeling
there should be another way.

NICK. Like enduring years of discomfort, you mean.

RACHEL (*laughing*). You think I should do it so you don't have to put up with me moaning any more?

NICK. I don't want you to be in pain.

RACHEL. Mr Quick-Fix.

Beat.

Anyway, it feels better. And I'd rather not... be poked about more than I have to, just now.

SIMON. Seems reasonable to me.

NICK. It's your wrist, Rachel, it's not open heart surgery.

RACHEL. Thank you, Simon. Nick thinks it's just another symptom of hormonal irrationality. Don't you, dear?

AMY. Oh, well, God forbid. Bloody men.

NICK. I didn't say that.

AMY (*to* NICK). It comes with the territory. Get used to it.

SIMON. Oh, I don't know...

NICK. All right, all right.

SIMON (*to* AMY). You were an utter delight, my dear. Both times. From beginning to end.

AMY. Watch it.

RACHEL. I think the point is that it's not about being pregnant. (*To* NICK.) It's about being realistic. Being honest.

They look at one another.

Pause.

NICK. Rachel thinks that by accepting the money, we've signed away our souls and sealed our various death warrants.

AMY. Ah.

RACHEL (*to* NICK). Don't do that...

NICK. She thinks it's bad karma.

RACHEL. No I don't.

Pause.

I'm sorry. Please don't be offended.

NICK *snorts.*

Well, it's a concern, isn't it? That things might be different. That we might feel... indebted... I mean, obviously we do feel indebted! On one level.

Beat.

But I wouldn't want it to change anything, that's all.

AMY. I don't see how it would.

SIMON (*holding up his hands*). No strings!

RACHEL *smiles.*

RACHEL. I know. I know.

Beat.

It's just if something came up... in the future. Something we didn't agree on...

NICK. Christ, Rachel!

RACHEL. I think it's worth talking about...

NICK. You're such a harbinger of doom!

RACHEL. ...Something small, I mean. But we felt we couldn't argue with you because you'd given us money and we were beholden to you, etcetera, etcetera...

SIMON. Hmmn. The lady may have a point, you know...

AMY. But you're not beholden to us! You wouldn't be! We're your friends, Rach. It's not like Simon and I are sitting here secretly expecting something in return. Honestly, I'm sure it'll be okay. We've known each other a long time and we're going into it with our eyes open... Besides, we're not Neanderthals – apart from Nick, obviously – if it does become a problem, we'll talk about it.

RACHEL. Yes.

Beat.

It's true. You're right.

Pause.

You just can't always tell, can you? What might happen. What people are capable of. Not you, I mean. Us. Anyone.

Beat.

What lurks within.

AMY (*laughing*). Well, when you put it like that…

SIMON (*holding up his hand as if to listen*). I can sense it. Brewing. Festering. Welling up… Look at them. Having fun! Putting it about! (*He pretends to swell with rage.*) THAT'S MY MONEY THEY'RE SPENDIIIIIINNNG…!

AMY. *Our* money.

SIMON. There you go. It's started. Dear God. We're *all* going to fall apart. Not just the friendship. Everything. Marriage. Relationship. The whole caboodle.

AMY. Shut up, Simon!

NICK. Yeah, shut up, Simon.

SIMON. I rest my case.

RACHEL. I know it'll be fine. I do. It's not as if we haven't been around.

NICK. Speak for yourself.

RACHEL (*laughing*). And, as you say, eyes open. Nick's right. I'm a doom merchant.

NICK *comes up behind her, puts his arms around her and bites her neck.*

AMY *looks away.*

NICK. Ah, but you're *my* doom merchant.

SIMON. I don't know. I vote we have a rethink.

NICK. Shut up and eat your tea.

SIMON. Right! That's it! I want my money back.

AMY. *Our* money.

SIMON flinches, pulling a face at NICK and RACHEL.

They all laugh.

Suspended beat.

SIMON looks mock-thoughtful.

SIMON. Mmm. I wonder, though. What would it be?

Pause.

The tipping point.

RACHEL (*grinning at him*). Our tragic downfall?

SIMON. I blame Amy.

RACHEL. Me too. Amy and Nick.

AMY. Wait a second! How come we get the blame?

RACHEL. You've known each other the longest.

SIMON. You have… a history.

NICK. We don't have a *history.*

RACHEL. Course you do. You can't know someone for as long as you two have without having a history.

AMY. So what does it mean, then? 'A history.'

SIMON. It means there are things that you two share or have shared from which we are excluded.

NICK. We don't exclude you. I don't exclude Rachel from anything.

He looks at AMY, who remains silent.

RACHEL. You don't actively exclude us, honey. It's not your fault. You talk. It's understandable.

NICK. But I don't exclude you!

RACHEL. That's what I'm saying. It's not conscious… This is silly. Cheese, anyone?

NICK. Wait, wait! Now it's silly. But all the stuff that came before – that wasn't silly? All the doom-and-gloom stuff. That wasn't silly.

SIMON. Easy, tiger…

RACHEL. Okay. I didn't mean anything by it. I don't want to start a row.

NICK. Oh Christ. It's not a row. This is not a row, Rachel. You're so fucking fatalistic. We'll be splitting up next.

AMY. Nick, come on. Just leave it. It doesn't matter.

Beat.

RACHEL. Well, it does, in fact. Because there are things we get left out of.

SIMON. She's right, you know. Arty stuff. All that business.

RACHEL. I end up feeling about this high sometimes. I don't do that to you. About music. Simon doesn't do it to you about the law.

NICK. That's because Simon doesn't care about the law! That's because Simon hates his job.

Silence.

SIMON. I don't hate my job.

NICK. Yes you do!

Pause.

NICK *looks around him for support.*

(*Laughing.*) Oh, come on, mate! Mr Hail-Fucker-Well-Met! It's a compromise and you know it. Christ. We're your friends. Be honest, for once in your sorry life. Beneath that huggy-bear exterior lurks a world of pain… You *hate* your fucking job!

Silence.

Secretly, Simon harbours thoughts of writing a novel of his own. Or a movie even! Go figure.

Long pause.

SIMON (*quietly*). And who gave you that idea, Nick?

Pause.

NICK *looks at* AMY *and realises he's been caught out.*

He gets up abruptly to fetch plates for the cheese.

The others sit in silence, without eye contact, for longer than is comfortable.

Eventually, NICK *opens his mouth to speak.*

RACHEL (*quickly*). I'm sorry. That was my fault.

Pause.

There's no reason why you two shouldn't share things. It's kind of… lovely.

Pause.

NICK (*to* RACHEL). I don't know, maybe we should… think about it. Maybe I should think about it. I don't want to make you feel stupid.

AMY (*shaking her head in agreement*). No.

NICK. That's… crap.

Pause.

AMY *and* RACHEL *turn to look at* SIMON. *He stares into his wine.*

Pause.

Blackout.

Scene Four

The same kitchen. Seven weeks later.

Both NICK *and* SIMON *are absent.* RACHEL *is big now.*
AMY *and* RACHEL *are setting the table, quite clearly in*
preparation for some form of Christmas dinner – a combination
of the traditional and the more exotic. A wine cooler is placed
in the middle of the table. At each setting they place a small
plate of gravadlax with capers.

This will be the most elaborate meal yet and the two women are
intent upon creating a masterpiece. Each article is positioned
with extreme care – napkins, additional wine glasses, holly,
crackers, fancy salt and pepper grinders. More than once, one
or other of them surreptitiously alters slightly what the other
has done.

As they move to and fro, they chat and laugh intermittently but
there is a slight tension in the air.

Occasionally, SIMON *appears in the doorway. He's on the*
mobile and is clearly irritated, in spite of which he still makes
an attempt at humour, rolling his eyes at them, banging his head
off the door jamb, etc.

RACHEL. Who's he talking to, anyway?

AMY. Mechanic. Who's a really nice guy, so I'm guessing the
    news isn't good.

RACHEL. Why? What's happened?

AMY (*snorts*). He was out to lunch yesterday with clients and
    managed to wrap the bumper around a rather large bollard
    that he swears blind wasn't there when he parked. So now
    he's blaming everyone but himself...

RACHEL. Including your very nice mechanic.

AMY. Exactly.

Silence.

Simon's actually quite sensitive.

RACHEL. Oh, definitely. I see that.

AMY *gives* RACHEL *an odd look.*

AMY. Maybe that's why he wrapped the car round a piece of street furniture – so keen to prove how much he loves his job.

Pause.

RACHEL. Amy… Nick just opens his mouth sometimes and… you wouldn't…

AMY. You forget how long I've known him.

They look at one another.

RACHEL. Of course.

Pause.

AMY. How's he been?

RACHEL. Oh. Not too bad. A bit stressed, I suppose. Things aren't going as fast as he'd like.

She smiles weakly.

And then other things are going too fast. It's funny. We still only just seem to be keeping our heads above water. Despite…

Pause.

RACHEL *is embarrassed. She laughs.*

It's amazing how it can get… eaten up.

AMY. Tell me about it.

Pause.

Has he been looking after you?

RACHEL. He's doing his best. I think. He was great initially. You know, after you told us… Well, you saw him – really excited. Writing loads. And he couldn't do enough for me. And then he drifted a bit. And now he just seems kind of… distracted.

Pause.

I mean, he's worried about money again. And his work, obviously. And… Oh, it'll sort itself out.

Pause.

He's not the best at the… nurturing stuff, is he?

There is the sound of a door opening and the clank of bottles.

AMY. Nope. There's never been much of the 'new man' about Nick.

NICK (*offstage*). Somebody call?

They laugh dryly.

NICK *enters.*

What are you two witches cackling about?

AMY. Twenty-first-century man.

RACHEL. His peaks and troughs.

NICK *dumps his carrier bags on the counter.*

AMY. We were comparing you and Si.

NICK *snorts dismissively and starts unpacking bottles of wine and champagne.*

NICK. You can hardly call Simon 'twenty-first century'. He's about as old school as they come.

SIMON *can be heard approaching.* AMY *looks* NICK *in the eye.*

AMY (*quietly*). Just don't start anything else.

NICK. Me?

SIMON *enters. He has a new, slightly manic quality about him.*

He's tense but making an attempt at jollity.

SIMON (*putting his arm around* NICK*'s shoulders*). Ho ho ho. What's all this?

He picks up one of the bottles to look at the label. He raises an eyebrow at what he sees.

You don't need to buy your way into our good books, you know, old boy!

NICK *freezes momentarily.* SIMON *appears oblivious.*

Beat.

RACHEL. Bad news about the car?

SIMON (*pulling a face at* AMY). One thousand and eighty flaming squids, I'm afraid, oh light of my life.

AMY. No!

NICK is opening a bottle of white wine.

SIMON. Curse those damned council workers and their efficiency.

RACHEL looks puzzled.

The bollard constructors. This looks incredible.

He approaches the table and dips his finger into a small dish.

AMY. How come so much?

SIMON. Pffff. (*Sucking his finger*). Some issue with the left-hand rear-flange-shaft-twoggle.

AMY. I thought it was the front bumper, for Christ's sake!

SIMON. Collateral damage.

RACHEL. And you trust him. Not to rip you off?

SIMON nods sorrowfully.

SIMON. It's the workhouse for us, I'm afraid, my love.

He picks a caper from one of the plates.

Ho-hum. 'Tis the season to be jolly. Good tidings and all that… so! (*He swings around, with his mouth full.*) Saint Nicholas! How's that book coming along? Got your draft in?

Pause.

NICK *looks at* RACHEL.

RACHEL. You've had a bit of a rough few weeks with it, haven't you, my love?

They all look at NICK.

SIMON. Oh?

Beat.

That's a shame.

Uneasy silence. SIMON *picks up the wine bottle that* NICK *has opened and heads for the table.*

Oh well. I suppose Rome wasn't built in a day. Shall we eat?

AMY *opens the oven and checks its contents. Closing it again, she picks up a carving knife and fork from the work surface. Meanwhile,* RACHEL, SIMON *and* NICK *settle themselves around the table.* SIMON *pours the wine, including a half glass for* RACHEL, *and places the bottle in the cooler. He raises his glass and waits for* AMY *to approach and pick up hers. She's still holding the carving knife and fork.*

Right then. Happy Christmas, one and all!

They all raise their glasses and respond.

They drink.

(*To* NICK, *indicating his glass with a wink.*) Nice choice. You come into some money?

RACHEL *and* AMY *laugh.* NICK *is furious. He drains his glass.*

AMY. Who's going to carve?

Pause.

NICK (*aggressively, to* SIMON). Isn't that your job?

SIMON *looks surprised.*

SIMON. I'm delighted to take a back seat, old boy.

RACHEL. I'll give it a go.

AMY *places the knife and fork in front of* RACHEL *and sits.*

SIMON *begins to eat the gravadlax.* AMY *and* RACHEL *follow suit.*

AMY. Nick seems to have you branded as old school, darling – some kind of avuncular nineteenth-century squire...

NICK *helps himself to more wine.*

RACHEL. We were discussing new men.

SIMON. Ah. It's all falling into place.

Pause.

RACHEL (*eating*). We don't think it's true, though. I mean, it's not a surface thing, is it? It's about sensibilities.

Pause.

NICK *is watching her, irritated.*

I don't think you're old school.

SIMON (*smiling*). You're sweet, angel, but I'm afraid he's right. He's blown my dirty little secret wide open. True blue through and through...

RACHEL. You're far too soft!

SIMON. And a boorish old bugger into the bargain.

RACHEL. But...

NICK. For fuck's sake, Rachel! The man is a self-confessed fascist. Can we not just drop it?

Silence.

NICK *drinks*.

The concept of the new man has always been just that,
anyway – a concept. He's a hologram. A projection of the
female psyche. A product of the female 'biological clock'.

SIMON. Oh, I don't know…

NICK. Exactly. Old school or not, it's the curse of early twenty-
first-century man that he's not permitted an opinion – so of
course you don't know.

RACHEL. I'm just saying I find it easy to tell him things.

NICK. That's why he's on the way out.

AMY. I don't understand.

NICK *waves his hand and begins to eat*.

NICK. It doesn't matter.

AMY. But who's on the way out?

NICK (*exploding*). You all seem to think it's so bloody easy!
Read the paper, scratch my bollocks, dash off a couple of
chapters between courses. I should be raking it in by now…

Pause.

NICK *resumes eating*.

We're engaged in a cultural reassessment.

AMY. Who's 'we'?

NICK. Me. Us. Everyone.

AMY. Christ, I hope not.

Pause.

NICK (*eating*). The model ain't working. Think about it. For
couples like us, what are the two single most significant
factors in our lives? One – Fertility. Or lack of. Two –
Money. Or lack of. The first is cited almost invariably as a
female dilemma. 'How late can I leave it? I've been told I

can have it all. Oh no, apparently I can't. D'oh. It appears they were lying after all…'

RACHEL *is staring at him. He doesn't look at her. As he talks, her horror increases.*

The second is generally regarded as a more universal and unisex problem. Debt. The Grim Reaper. It's the flip side of its own particular coin. A metropolis built on quicksand… 'Neither a borrower nor a lender be.' Good advice. It appears we omitted to listen.

AMY. And the reassessment?

NICK. That the two issues are inextricably intertwined… That for men like me, the current status quo is… unhelpful. And that we deserve some sympathy.

He takes a large swig of wine.

AMY. Ah, now we're getting to it. How so?

RACHEL. Could we change the subject, please?

NICK (*ignoring her*). Look at you two. (*He indicates* AMY *and* SIMON.) Society tells us we should be more like you. Problem. Rachel is… getting on. She wants babies. *I* am not rich – something of a late starter. I do, however, have potential. But unfortunately for me my potential to achieve is in direct conflict with Rachel's ability to *con*ceive. Thus, I'm forced to take a back seat because the 'clock is ticking'. And I lose out on all counts. My masculinity is undermined. By the debt in which I find myself, by my inability to make good that debt and by the even deeper debt into which I am destined to be plunged by my progeny. My talent remains latent and disregarded.

AMY. That's such a load of old bollocks, Nick.

NICK. Nail on the head, Amy. Your 'new man' is in fact a eunuch.

Silence.

Don't look at me like that. I refuse to be lambasted for this.
I'm not some nineties-throwback-Nick-Hornby-
commitment-phobic.

AMY. No, that's what you were *in* the nineties.

NICK. Yes, and I've moved on. I've joined ranks. I've grown
up. But my point is that now I'm being penalised for it. If I
want to be with Rachel – (*To* RACHEL.) which I *do* – I'm
forced to accept that my time is no longer my own. That I'm
now working to someone else's agenda.

Pause.

NICK *continues to eat.*

It's not a big deal.

Silence.

AMY. So, it's Rachel's fault?

SIMON. A cultural reassessment, eh?

RACHEL. I have an agenda?

NICK. Oh God. Here we go. That's not what I'm saying. This is
exactly it! It always comes back around to you!

Beat.

Of *course* I'm not saying that. I'm simply trying to express a
miniscule frustration at the fact that…

AMY. That you're disempowered? That women rule.

NICK (*indicating* AMY *and* RACHEL). That this problem is
considered exclusive to you. All this career-baby stuff. I'm
pointing out that we're suffering too.

AMY. Unbelievable.

SIMON. Who's 'we'?

NICK. Well, not you. Obviously. You're the archetype.

SIMON. Am I now? How lovely.

NICK. The nature of your sacrifice is different. You've followed the old-school model. Fifties' values. Accepting the role of breadwinner.

AMY. Oh, how gracious. You allow that that's a sacrifice then?

SIMON. I don't think it's a sacrifice.

NICK. You're conditioned to think that.

AMY. For God's sake. You make him sound like an automaton.

NICK. I just mean it wouldn't make a difference to Simon – not so much of a difference – at what point you decided to have kids.

They stare at him.

At what point the two of you decided.

He glances nervously at RACHEL.

Look. I'm not claiming an exclusive right to suffering here! I just want an acknowledgement that we're all being pushed around. By society. By one another. And that some of us get burned along the way.

Beat.

The pressure is on me to earn.

Pause.

AMY. Maybe you could just buy less cheese.

NICK *and* RACHEL *look at her.*

Beat.

AMY *gets up abruptly and goes to check the oven again.*

Pause.

RACHEL (*to* NICK). I've never forced you into anything.

NICK. Christ! It's not about you forcing me! I'm not some kind of monster. I want you to be happy. I just don't want to be a… skint underachiever any more. I want to be happy too!

There is silence. They've all stopped eating.

RACHEL *is holding on to her tummy.*

RACHEL. I see.

Pause.

She looks at SIMON.

So. Maybe I was right after all.

NICK. What?

NICK *swings around to look at* SIMON.

What? Right about what?

NICK *looks back at* RACHEL, *who holds his gaze.*

RACHEL. To be worried.

Beat.

About telling you.

NICK. Telling me?

RACHEL. About how you'd take it.

NICK. You what?

RACHEL. Whether you'd be *happy.*

Pause.

NICK. Wait. You discussed it with *him*?

Beat.

Our baby?

Silence.

What the fuck? Before me? He knew before me? (*To* SIMON.) You fucking hypocrite…

RACHEL. I'd rather you didn't take it out on Simon, please.

NICK. …You already knew…

Beat.

How long?

RACHEL. I was scared, Nick.

NICK. HOW LONG?

SIMON. Not long…

RACHEL. Just after the test.

NICK. Wow!

He looks at SIMON.

Quite the Renaissance man, aren't we?

SIMON. I'm sorry?

NICK. Our Confessor now as well as our Mighty Benefactor.

RACHEL. Oh, don't be stupid.

NICK (*to* RACHEL). Are you sure I'm the father?

She looks at him with hatred.

RACHEL. And you're surprised I didn't talk to you.

NICK. Of what? Scared of what?

RACHEL. Scared that you wouldn't want it! That you wouldn't even… believe in it.

NICK (*violently*). 'Believe in it'?

RACHEL *jumps.*

What the hell does that mean? It wa… isn't the bloody… tooth fairy! 'Believe in it.'

AMY. Nick.

He looks at AMY.

NICK. And all that crap! About me and Amy! Sharing secrets. When all along Mr Bountiful here is playing therapist to my wife!

RACHEL. Oh, don't be so melodramatic.

SIMON. Calm down, old man. We never accused you of sharing *secrets*.

Beat.

AMY. You did, actually.

Pause.

You implied that we talk about everything.

RACHEL *turns on her.*

RACHEL. And that's not true?

AMY *is uneasy.*

AMY. Of course it's not.

RACHEL. So you two didn't discuss this baby? Not at all? Not my 'history', nothing? I'm sorry, Amy. I'm loath to drag you into this, but do you honestly expect us to believe that?

AMY. I beg your pardon?

AMY *glances nervously at* NICK.

RACHEL. I just find it kind of... implausible, that you wouldn't have talked about it. Knowing the facts. Knowing Nick as you do. It must have been... tough to resist.

AMY *is silent.*

I mean, he must have been worried. About going through it all again.

Beat.

Don't you think?

AMY. Yes. I assume so.

RACHEL. Well, you're probably right. You've known him so long.

NICK. Oh, for fuck's sake.

AMY. I've never...

RACHEL. So tell me then. Considered opinion. (*Indicates the size of her tummy.*) Do you think he actually expected this?

AMY. What?

RACHEL. This! To get to this stage? In fact, did you? Did either of you expect it?

AMY. Yes, of course.

RACHEL. So you did talk about it?

AMY. That's not what I'm saying… I…

RACHEL. Because I imagined it being quite a shock, I must say.

AMY. I meant me. I expected it.

RACHEL. I had the impression that nobody *really* thought it was going to happen.

SIMON (*soothingly*). Of course we did.

RACHEL. Oh, well, that's reassuring. Nick?

NICK is silent. RACHEL turns to look at AMY.

AMY. Look…

Beat.

I don't know what Nick thought.

Beat.

Because we didn't talk about it.

Pause.

RACHEL. Oh.

Long silence.

NICK (*quietly*). We were worried about you, Rachel.

RACHEL. Ah.

She turns to AMY, who is mortified.

Pause.

SIMON. Okay. Maybe we all need to take a step back…

AMY (*to* RACHEL). I've never been anything other than supportive.

RACHEL looks from AMY to NICK and back.

RACHEL. True. You've always been terribly concerned.

SIMON. I mean, it's not a crime, is it? To share secrets… confidences… with someone who isn't your lover…

RACHEL. No, Simon. It's not a crime.

Beat.

So. What about now?

Beat.

How do we rate my chances – (*Touching her tummy.*) our chances, now?

NICK. Rachel, stop.

Pause.

RACHEL. Big changes in store, eh? If we do manage. To hang on.

She looks around at them. No one meets her eye.

Sorry. You probably haven't discussed that either.

Pause.

I suppose you'll need to come to us more often…

Beat.

AMY (*coldly*). That's never been a problem.

RACHEL. Oh. Right.

SIMON (*gently*). Of course, we know things are going to change, Rachel.

Beat.

RACHEL. Ha. I feel quite Christmassy all of a sudden!

NICK. Rach…

RACHEL. Nick. It's good to talk, isn't it? Get things out in the open. And don't get me wrong, I'm delighted you had an outlet.

AMY. What?

SIMON. Okay, now I think that's a bit harsh, don't you?

RACHEL. Is it? I don't mean to be harsh, Si.

Beat.

You understand. I know you do.

SIMON *looks uncomfortable*.

But then maybe you find it a comfort to know that whatever happens to you, Amy always has Nick…

AMY (*exploding*). What the hell? Nick and I are friends!

RACHEL. I suppose what it is… is maybe I'm just intrigued…

Pause.

Intrigued as to why – given that you were all clearly so worried about me – none of you would think of talking to me about it? Directly. You know.

NICK. That's not fair.

RACHEL. Isn't it?

AMY. No, it bloody well isn't! We've always been there for you, Rachel!

RACHEL. That's funny.

AMY. Every time. For years now…

RACHEL. See, I don't recall you being there at all.

AMY. Tiptoeing around… trying…

RACHEL. Not one of you. Not the first time, at the flat…

AMY.…to say the right thing – desperate not to say…

RACHEL. Not in the changing room…

AMY. …the wrong thing. Coping with your moods…

RACHEL. *Certainly* not at the school…

AMY. Christ, you're surely not…

RACHEL. When I'd walked a mile and a half to pick up *your* child –

AMY. …holding *us* responsible now!

RACHEL. – because once again *you* couldn't make it!

Pause.

AMY. I don't have to listen to this shit.

RACHEL. Or afterwards, Ames. What about afterwards? I could swear you weren't there then. As I sobbed and screamed and scrubbed the blood from my hands. Over and over. Rinsing, rinsing it from my hair, smearing it from my face… from my eyelashes.

Beat.

I… simply… don't… remember… you… being… there.

Pause.

I don't suppose you've ever wrung your own blood out of a piece of clothing? Scraped your own child from under your fingernails? Amazing.

Pause.

I thought my heart had burst.

Silence.

AMY. Rachel, I…

RACHEL (*gently*). Do you have any notion what it was like for me to be with you? How I could barely walk into a room with you breastfeeding Rosie? How it made me feel physically sick to see a pregnant woman across the street, on a bus, at the cinema…

AMY. I...

RACHEL. No, of course you don't. Because no one does, do they? And so no one knows what to do – after the second, the third time – with all that grief. That appalling, inconvenient grief. No one knows what to do, so they don't do anything. They stop saying how many people it happens to, how unlikely it is to happen again, how sorry they are and yet how temporary that's bound to be... in fact, they just stop talking to you at all. You're transformed... into a kind of barren psychotic leper floundering in a mire of swollen bellies and other people's oestrogen. And d'you know, the worst thing is you start to expect it yourself. Every time you bend. Every time you stand up too suddenly. Every time you go to piss. That little creature. Little arms, little legs... Drowning... Drowning in a sea of your own blood.

Silence.

AMY. I'm so sorry.

RACHEL. I read a beautiful description once. 'Born silently.' Our son, Joshua, born silently at twenty weeks.

Beat.

It sounds so serene, doesn't it?

Pause.

That's not been my experience.

NICK. I did try to talk to you. Lots of times. You forget.

RACHEL. No, you didn't. No, you didn't, Nick. That wasn't talking. All you tried to do was convince me that to have a baby wasn't really what I wanted. Because you didn't think I could. You had no faith.

Pause.

And I think maybe that suited you rather better.

Beat.

NICK. All I want, all I've ever wanted, is for you to be happy. And I think I've done my best to achieve that. It's just that I have things that I want too… Things I want to do. Things that get…

AMY. Aborted?

They turn to look at AMY.

Pause.

You're not seriously comparing writing your poxy novel to carrying a baby? You're not comparing an extended coffee break to having a miscarriage?

SIMON. Now. Folks. Please. (*To* AMY.) Come on… I really don't think that's what Nick's saying…

AMY. Have you been listening to any of this?

SIMON. Of course I have. I just don't think that Nick's equating his 'creation' with Rachel's, that's all.

NICK. Course I'm bloody not.

RACHEL. Yes he is. That's exactly what he's doing.

SIMON. Let's not start again, eh?

AMY (*to* SIMON). I don't understand why you're defending him.

NICK. Anyway, it's not her creation, it's ours.

SIMON (*firmly*). I'm not defending him… I just think we need to… keep things in perspective.

Pause.

NICK. And thus spake Solomon.

SIMON. Let's eat.

They look at him, blankly.

Pause.

Slowly AMY *rises, followed by* RACHEL *and then* SIMON.

In silence, the three of them clear the table and bring out the next course. It is hugely elaborate, a banquet, piled high on the table – a glistening roast, vegetables, stuffing, sauces.

For a long time, all that can be heard is the clink of metal against china, glass against glass, china against wood, liquid being poured, etc.

The silence becomes more and more intolerable.

Throughout, NICK *remains seated, watching. Ostentatiously he helps himself to wine.*

AMY *and* SIMON *sit, passing plates around, serving up vegetables as* RACHEL *carves.*

From hereon in, nobody eats a morsel.

NICK. It's like the game.

Pause.

'Simon Says'.

Pause.

Nick says stick a fork up your arse.

They ignore him. He peers at each of them in turn.

Ooh. You're all too good.

SIMON *picks up the bottle of wine and helps the others to some before starting to help himself.* NICK *realises his faux pas.*

Oops.

SIMON (*lowering the bottle*). Okay, Nick. Do you have something you want to say to me?

NICK *looks around at the others and back at* SIMON.

Pause.

NICK. Sorry, Dad.

Pause.

SIMON *resumes pouring wine for himself.*

Well, this must be galling.

AMY *looks at* NICK *in disgust.*

I mean, basically, it's what you do, isn't it?

AMY. Why are you doing this?

NICK (*to* SIMON). Settle arguments.

AMY. Why are you taking this out on us?

NICK. It's how you make your mega-bucks.

Pause.

AMY. Look. We understand that you're hurting. We do. But this is between you. The pair of you.

Silence.

RACHEL (*quietly*). It's not, though, is it? Not any more.

Silence.

Whose idea was it? Just out of interest. To give us the money? (*To* NICK.) We think it was Amy's, don't we?

Pause.

AMY *and* SIMON *look at one another.*

AMY. And what are you saying? That it was a bad thing? Some kind of power trip? You seemed pretty grateful at the time.

Beat.

An act of pure generosity, you said.

NICK. And you said no strings.

AMY. So?

SIMON *rests his head on his hands.*

RACHEL. Oh, come on, Ames, you know what we mean.

AMY. No. Actually, I don't.

RACHEL. *Why* did you give us the money?

Beat.

Simon?

SIMON. You know why.

RACHEL. Because we're your dear friends and you love us.

AMY. We wanted to help you.

NICK. Because we couldn't help ourselves?

AMY. I'm sorry now that we did.

RACHEL. Thing is. You guys love all that stuff, don't you…

NICK (*to* SIMON). Checking up on me. My progress.

RACHEL. Holding things together. Being in charge.

NICK. Keeping track of your investment.

RACHEL. Telling us how much cheese to buy.

Beat.

AMY. I'm allowed to say what I think.

NICK. What, because you've bought the right?

AMY. Because that's what friends do, Nick.

RACHEL. Is it?

AMY. Yes. It is. Especially when people clearly can't work it out for themselves.

NICK. Ah! You were saving us from ourselves.

AMY. Oh, get real, Nick. You're having a baby. When are you going to grow up?

RACHEL. Amy. We're poorer than you. That's all.

AMY. And has it not occurred to you, Rachel, that there could be a reason for that?

Beat.

RACHEL. That we don't have Simon to support us?

AMY. How dare you? How dare you blame us for your failings when all we've done has been for your benefit!

SIMON (*warning*). Amy.

AMY. What? You won't say it, so I'm not supposed to?

SIMON *bows his head.*

Why not, Simon? Why not let's share? Everyone else seems to be! After all, I think we're both pretty clear on what the problem is, aren't we, my love? I seem to remember you nailing it quite precisely, in fact. The problem is not that they're poor, per se. That's right, yeah? The problem is actually much simpler than that. The problem – naming no names – is that one of them is so up his own arse that he thinks that real work is beneath him and the other has allowed herself, what was it…? To become so consumed by her own misery that she no longer takes responsibility for anything else!

RACHEL *looks at* SIMON.

Silence.

RACHEL (*quietly, to* AMY). You little bitch.

They look at her in shock.

AMY. And yet they just keep on spending.

RACHEL. You snobby, self-satisfied little bitch.

Pause.

The perfect life, eh, Amy?

Long pause.

I do get how hard it must be for you, you know.

AMY. What are you talking about?

NICK (*to* SIMON). So, what happens next then, boss?

RACHEL. Watching it all unfold.

NICK. When it gets real? When a draft gets accepted. When it's published.

AMY. You know nothing about me.

RACHEL. Accepting the changes. Letting go…

AMY. There's something wrong with you, Rachel.

RACHEL. …of what you *really* want.

NICK. Come on, mate! What if I sell the screen rights? What if I make some proper money? What then?

RACHEL. Of who you really want.

SIMON *is watching* AMY.

AMY. I would stop if I were you.

RACHEL. Realising what you've got to lose. What happens when we *do* have the perfect baby. Me and Nick?

NICK. Do you two have shares?

RACHEL. It's like a fairy tale!

Beat.

(*Turning to* NICK.) Maybe we should give them our first-born!

AMY. You shouldn't even be together!

They all look at her.

Silence.

She looks around.

Oh, come on. It's so bloody obvious.

Beat.

You're not right for him, Rachel. You and your suffering. Your interminable suffering. You're just another excuse. You allow him to fail.

Beat.

Nick doesn't need you. He doesn't want the things you want.

Beat.

People like Nick need air. They need fire.

Beat.

She looks at SIMON.

They need passion.

Long pause.

NICK. Amy, Rachel is my passion.

AMY *throws up her hands, rises abruptly and begins furiously to clear the uneaten meal from the table.*

AMY. This is…!

She shakes her head and carries a pile of dishes over to the work surface, flings them down and heads back for more.

They watch her in shock as she goes back and forth.

SIMON (*quietly*). Unacceptable.

NICK *starts to giggle.*

NICK. What?

SIMON *turns slowly towards him as* AMY *approaches the table once more.*

SIMON. This… is UNACCEPTABLE!

As he shouts the word, he overturns the table with all his might, sending the remainder of its contents flying in all directions. Plates of food crash to the floor.

NICK *leaps to his feet like a sulky teenager but is unsure what to do next and remains rooted to the spot.*

They look in shocked silence at the pile of food and broken china.

(*Quietly furious.*) Yes, it was Amy's idea! To give you the money. To help you out. Pure and simple. Because she thinks the world of you. Both of you. And whatever your fears or misconceptions or… (*He looks directly at* AMY.) expectations are around that, I would strongly advise that you set them aside!

RACHEL *gets to her feet, as if in a trance, and picks up the carving knife. With her other hand, she picks up her plate.*

NICK. Are you threatening us?

SIMON *ignores him.*

SIMON. Amy's idea. I agreed. But do you know what? You don't have the monopoly on lack of faith, Nick.

Beat.

Checking up on my 'investment'.

RACHEL *moves to the pile of food and broken crockery.*

There are things I don't believe in too, you know.

NICK. I don't know what you're talking about.

SIMON. Rachel, I'm sorry you're in pain.

RACHEL *bends and begins slowly to scrape the food and crockery onto her plate with the knife.*

The last thing I want is to make things harder for you than they already are. But I think we all understand…

He looks at NICK.

…that Nick's never going to finish that novel. It's never going to happen…

Beat.

Not because of anyone else…

NICK (*genuinely shocked*). You fucking wanker…

SIMON. Not even because he has no commitment, no sense of responsibility, a mediocre talent…

NICK. You cunt! I…

NICK *launches himself toward* SIMON, *flinging a chair aside as he does so, but hesitates as he gets close.*

SIMON. But because he's lazy. Because he's a coward.

SIMON *moves towards him so that their faces are close.*

And because he has no pride.

NICK *makes a grab for* SIMON *but he's too slow. With a mighty heave,* SIMON *sends him flying across the kitchen floor. He crashes into a cupboard, where he stays slumped, covering his eyes with his hand.*

You're asking me to question my motives. Well, here's your answer. Truth is… left to my own devices, I probably wouldn't have given you the money in the first place.

Beat.

If the tables were turned… I certainly wouldn't have taken it.

NICK *is sobbing into his hand.*

So maybe that makes you right. That I've sold out.

He crouches in front of NICK.

(*Very quietly.*) But do you know what, Nicholas, I believe that however hard they make it, if you love someone, if you *have* loved, there is a debt. And if you turn your back on that debt…

AMY *looks in horror at* SIMON.

A barely audible whimper from RACHEL.

AMY *drags her eyes from* SIMON *to* RACHEL.

RACHEL *kneels on the floor, surrounded by broken crockery, the knife still clutched in her hand. She holds her other hand low on her abdomen.*

…then you don't deserve to have them.

One after the other, SIMON *and* NICK *turn to follow* AMY*'s gaze.*

RACHEL *is still.*

The three of them stare at her in shock.

Blackout.

Epilogue

The same kitchen. Three months later. AMY *is alone. She stands at the sink, scrubbing a chopping board. Her movements are seamless but unaccustomedly slow.*

The kitchen is immaculate, save for one end of the table, which is supported by a trestle. There is no music and no evidence of food.

A single brown-paper bag lies beside AMY *on the counter.*

She dries the chopping board and puts it away. From upstairs comes the muffled sound of voices. She pauses for a moment to listen.

From a cupboard, she takes four plates and four tumblers, which she places on the table. She fetches four sets of knives and forks from a drawer. She pours salt into a bowl and brings it to the table along with a pepper grinder, a bottle of olive oil and a second, empty bowl. Finally she unwraps the brown-paper bag to reveal a rough, country loaf. She puts it on a breadboard and places it in the middle of the table.

She surveys the room, appears satisfied, and sits.

Silence.

Eventually there is the sound of a door closing up above and footsteps on the stairs. AMY *doesn't move.*

NICK *enters. He looks nervous but it's instantly apparent that there is a change in him. He radiates a new confidence. He's happy.*

He stands in the doorway.

AMY *turns to face him.*

Pause.

NICK. Feeding.

Beat.

No telling how long, I'm afraid. Likes his grub.

AMY. Simon's not back yet anyway.

NICK enters but is unsure where to go and stops.

Sit. If you want.

He sits uneasily.

Pause.

NICK. Big man working late then?

AMY. He went to see his father.

NICK. Oh! Right.

Pause.

AMY. He's taking the kids there at the weekend.

NICK. Blimey.

AMY. Blimey.

Beat.

Have you two spoken yet?

NICK. No.

Silence.

AMY. I thought he might have... contacted.

NICK watches her.

Beat.

NICK (*gently*). It's good to see you, Ames.

She looks at him across the table.

Thanks for doing this.

AMY *shrugs.*

AMY. Thanks for calling.

They smile at one another.

So. You seem…

NICK. More well-balanced?

Beat.

More in control? Better looking?

AMY. Taller.

NICK (*grinning*). He's so beautiful.

AMY. He is.

NICK. And at last I've got them home. Same rush all over again.

Beat.

The second coming.

Beat.

We took him to Kew yesterday. First family outing.

Beat.

It was shit. He hated it. Said 'arboretums are gay'.

AMY *smiles gently.*

Pause.

I do know I'm not the first. Honest.

Silence.

AMY. How's… the other stuff?

He laughs.

NICK. There's other stuff?

Beat.

Oh, you know. Thought maybe I should… knuckle down a bit. Under the circumstances.

Beat.

I rooted out some of those articles. The ones from last year that… weren't quite finished. Bit of a tweak here and there. Turns out they really like them – capturing the zeitgeist and all that shit.

Pause.

Talk of giving me a column.

There is a sound from upstairs. NICK is suddenly alert, listening.

Pause.

AMY. You know they closed the gallery?

NICK. Huh?

Beat.

Your gallery?

AMY. Yeah. My gallery.

NICK. Why?

AMY *shrugs. She rubs her thumb and forefinger together to indicate cash.*

NICK. Shit.

AMY. So. I'm a lady of leisure. A kept woman.

Beat.

NICK. What are you going to do?

AMY. Well… I thought maybe I could retrieve my children from the workhouse. Spend some 'quality time' with them.

Pause.

And I've started painting again.

NICK. Seriously? Ames, that's great. Good for you.

The sound of movement upstairs.

Aha. There she is, now.

They listen.

That's pretty quick, actually. Maybe he's not settling. Strange place and all that.

He strains to hear.

Perhaps I should go up. Help out.

He stands. There is the sound of a key in the front door.

NICK *stops dead. The door opens. Footsteps.*

SIMON *appears, framed in the doorway. He looks at* NICK.

Their eyes lock. The hunter and the hunted.

SIMON *strides into the room as* NICK *leaps towards him. They look as if they might clash.*

They speak simultaneously.

SIMON. Nicholas!

NICK. Mate!

They shake hands, clap one another on the back. It's not the same as it was. SIMON *is formal, like a man greeting a colleague.*

SIMON. Yes. Good to see you. Congratulations, congratulations.

They pause, unsure what to do next. AMY *looks on.*

Have I missed the little chap?

NICK. He's... having his tea.

SIMON. Ah. Uh-huh. Man after my own heart.

SIMON *takes off his coat.*

NICK *indicates the door.*

NICK. I was... uh...

SIMON. Excellent.

He gives AMY *a peck on the cheek and takes his coat out into the hall.*

NICK *sits.*

SIMON *re-enters and heads for the wine rack.*

Good.

He selects a bottle, fetches the corkscrew and begins to open the wine.

So. How's... it all going?

NICK. Great. Yeah. Loving it. Loving the dad thing.

SIMON. Ah. Aha.

NICK. And working away... You?

SIMON *is struggling with the cork. He inspects it carefully then tries again. It's clearly disintegrating.*

SIMON. Yes. Ticking over, yes. Thanks.

AMY. Simon's been offered a partnership.

SIMON *opens up the penknife attachment and attempts to dig out some of the loose pieces of cork.*

NICK. Really?

Beat.

Really? Amazing. Wow.

SIMON'*s hand slips and he cuts his finger on the penknife.*

SIMON. Dammit.

AMY *gets up and goes to the sink. She turns on the tap for* SIMON. *He holds his finger under it.* AMY *inspects the cut, fetches a plaster for him, dries it and puts the plaster on.*

Thanks.

He goes back to excavating the cork.

NICK. So. What... does that mean? What would it mean?

SIMON *shrugs*.

SIMON. More dosh. Bigger workload… The usual.

Pause.

Going to eat into my time a bit, but… Heigh-ho.

Beat.

You've heard about Amy's career change.

NICK. Yeah. She was saying. It's great.

Beat.

SIMON. Uh-huh. Gotta support the arts, eh? Troubled times and all that.

Silence.

NICK. Absolutely.

Silence.

Upstairs there is the sound of a door opening.

SIMON. Aha.

NICK. There she is.

Pause.

There are footsteps on the stairs.

They listen.

RACHEL *appears in the doorway, holding a baby monitor.*

They look at her.

SIMON. The Lady Madonna.

He places the unopened bottle by the hob and goes to kiss her on the cheek.

Hello, my dear. You look well.

RACHEL. Thank you.

Pause.

You too.

She plugs in the baby monitor.

SIMON. How's the lamb?

RACHEL. He's fine, thanks. Out like a light.

She fiddles with the controls. They listen to the static.

SIMON. Drink?

RACHEL *hesitates.*

RACHEL. I will.

AMY *fetches a new bottle from the wine rack and places it on the table.*

RACHEL *sits.*

SIMON *fetches the corkscrew and begins opening the second bottle of wine.*

AMY *checks the oven.*

She comes to the table and sits. NICK *moves behind* RACHEL *and begins to massage her shoulders. She doesn't respond.*

SIMON. Tired?

RACHEL *nods.*

AMY. Just you wait.

Pause.

NICK *gives up the massage and seats himself at the table.*

SIMON *pours wine into each of the four tumblers.*

NICK. What's it going to be then, Ames?

AMY. Stew.

Beat.

Got my timings wrong. Won't be long.

SIMON. Talk amongst yourself.

They laugh politely.

AMY *breaks a chunk off the loaf.*

She pours olive oil from the bottle into the empty bowl and adds a hefty pinch of salt.

She dips her bread in the oil and takes a bite, wincing slightly as she does so.

The others follow suit.

They drink.

They eat more bread in silence.

AMY. So, Nick. You want to see my etchings?

They look at one another in shock. NICK *glances at* RACHEL. *She gives him a small smile.*

NICK. I thought you'd never ask.

He bends to kiss RACHEL *and follows* AMY *from the room.*

SIMON *and* RACHEL *listen to the footsteps through the baby monitor.* NICK *and* AMY*'s conversation is indecipherable.*

Silence.

RACHEL. He doesn't know you were at the hospital.

Pause.

SIMON. Have you decided what you're going to do?

RACHEL *rests her head in her hands.*

Pause.

RACHEL. I spoke to my mum. She managed to control her elation. Barely. Offered to buy me a flat if necessary. If there was any problem selling the house.

Beat.

Her generosity knows no bounds all of a sudden.

SIMON. Blood and water, eh?

RACHEL. I don't know. I just don't know.

Pause.

Nick seems to have reconciled something. In his own head. Maybe that's enough.

Pause.

I'm sorry, Si. For everything.

SIMON. You'd be missed.

Pause.

RACHEL. What about you?

SIMON. Huh. We'll plough on. No need to upset the bairns.

Pause.

No need.

The sound through the baby monitor of NICK *and* AMY *returning.*

RACHEL *and* SIMON *listen to the footsteps on the stairs.*

RACHEL (*quietly*). I just don't feel... excited any more.

SIMON *nods.*

NICK *and* AMY *enter.*

RACHEL *looks at* NICK *inquiringly.*

NICK. Can you credit it!

Pause.

I do believe Amy's going to be famous.

They all look at AMY.

SIMON. Ah! Jolly good. Just what we need.

AMY *goes to the oven. Silence as she checks the contents.*

AMY *removes the covered casserole from the oven and carries it to the table. She stands, holding it.*

RACHEL *rises mechanically, fetches the chopping board and puts it on the table.* AMY *places the casserole on top of it.*

RACHEL *sits.*

AMY *fetches a ladle which she puts beside the casserole.*

AMY *sits.*

NICK *remains standing.*

They look at the dish.

AMY. It's going to have to do.

They look at one another.

SIMON. Right. Shall we eat?

Pause.

Suddenly, NICK *begins to dig frantically in his pockets. He's clearly nervous.*

The others watch him, puzzled.

NICK. What I was saying, Simon, to Ames. Earlier on. I've been... bucking the trend a bit recently. Workwise, that is. Not the novel. Clearly. Clearly not the novel. But this and that. Bits and pieces. You know. So...

NICK *produces a wad of crumpled notes which he places on the table next to the casserole.*

So this is for you. For the two of you. Drop in the ocean, really, but... First instalment.

SIMON, AMY *and* RACHEL *stare in shock at the money on the table.*

Of the repayments.

Silence.

Sounds through the baby monitor.

SIMON. There's really no need, old man.

The baby begins to cry.

RACHEL *and* NICK *look at one another.* RACHEL *starts to stand.*

NICK. I'll go.

Beat.

Maybe I could bring him down.

He touches SIMON *hesitantly on the shoulder.*

Introduce you.

SIMON *and* RACHEL *exchange glances.*

NICK *heads for the door.*

He pauses, turns in the doorway.

Thing is. I'd... really appreciate it, mate. If you would take the money.

He leaves.

They sit looking at the pile of notes.

NICK*'s rapid footsteps are heard on the stairs. Through the monitor, he can be heard approaching the bed.*

NICK (*voice-over*). Sssshhh. Sssh.

The sound of the baby being picked up. His crying ceases as NICK *begins to sing very quietly.*

You are my sunshine, my only sunshine...

Beat.

You make me happy...

AMY *reaches slowly for the money.*

When skies are grey...

She begins to uncrumple the notes, one by one, pressing them flat and piling them one on top of the other.

The lights begin to fade.

You'll never know, dear... How much I love you. So please don't take...

Pause.

Blackout.

The End.